MW00531703

5/11/2021

To Morqyn And Sean

Best wishes and enjoy this book

Ronald Harrill

# CHILDREN OF GENESIS

THE BLACK NATIONS IN THE OLD TESTAMENT

RONALD HARRILL

**Writing and Research:** Ronald Harrill for R. Harrill Enterprises 2311 Holly Lane, Shelby, NC 28150

**Artwork and Illustrations, Design, Page Layout, Editing and Art Direction:** Michael O. Johnson for A Touch Of Omari, 206 Worthington St., Shelby, NC 28150



**ISBN:** 978-0-9883082-0-6

Library of Congress Cataloging-in-Publication Data

"Children of Genesis" published in the United States by:
R. Harrill Enterprises
2311 Holly Lane
Shelby, NC 28150

Printed and manufactured in the United States by:
Worzalla Publishing Co.
3535 Jefferson St.
Stevens Point, WI 54481
(715) 344-9600
www.worzalla.com

Unless stated otherwise, all Old Testament quotations come from The Holy Bible, King James Version. Cambridge Edition: 1769; King James Bible Online, 2020.

# DEDICATION

To three men who helped to shape my life:

Samuel Canaan (Pinky) McCombs
James N. (Sonny) Byrd Jr.
Reverend Calvin Johnson

And to my wife Denise and
sons Kenyon, Aaron and Nathan

# Contents

# My Journey

I often have discussed events that shaped my life and propelled me on this never-ending journey of research on Africa and people of African ancestry. It's been a lifelong journey supported with a continuous passion for researching and exploring the wonders of our historical past.

As I look back at my life, I see a series of events and circumstances that contributed to my cultural and personal development. I certainly did not understand the big picture as these events occurred, but I now see them as the foundation that helped me arrive at the point of writing this book.

In October 1956, my godmother gave me my first Bible. I was an inquisitive 6-year-old, first-grade student at an all-Negro segregated school in Shelby, North Carolina. The Bible had a white leathery cover, which caught my eye because it was different from the standard black cover Bibles in our church.

For the next six years, I carried my Bible to Sunday school and church. I initially couldn't read all the words, but I constantly looked at the pictures contained in the holy book. Along with my formal education, the Bible was the primary source of my learning. It helped me learn how to read, form sentences and pronounce new words.

In my earlier years, the pictures in the Bible dominated my thoughts. As I read and listened to stories of Adam and Eve in the Garden of Eden, Noah and the Great Flood and Moses with the 10 Commandments, these people were my early-life heroes. Even though all characters in the pictures were white, that concept didn't bother me because I learned that most — if not all — biblical characters were strong, brave white people. I can't recall any times that I questioned the validity of those pictures.

I belonged to a warm, caring old southern black church founded in 1867. We believed and taught members that everything in the Bible was true and correct — in other words, "Don't question it." Even during my teenage years, I simply didn't dream or fantasize that there could have been black people participating in significant biblical events.

## My Early Cultural Platform

I spent the first 15 years of my life as a second-class citizen in the United States of America. Growing up during the civil rights movement of the 1950s and 1960s, we simply didn't have full rights and freedom that comes from citizenship. We lived in designated neighborhoods reserved for Negro people (yes, black Americans were called "Negroes" during that period).

We attended all-Negro schools, we could not sit down and eat at local restaurants and we had to sit upstairs in seats allocated for colored/Negro people when attending the local theaters.

My official birth certificate recorded my race as "colored," and the colored designation also included both of my parents. I heard the term "colored people" often as a child, so this didn't bother me at all. I saw the word "colored" on public bathrooms and water fountains reserved for our people.

Somewhere near the third grade, around 1958, I began to hear people calling us Negroes. I began to read and use the term "Negro" as I progressed in school, and that was a good experience. That designation lasted until maybe the mid-1960s when a new, phenomenal cultural impact covered the landscape — and then we became known as black people.

The year 1964 was memorable with the passing of the Civil Rights Act that mentioned we were now first-class citizens in the USA. It produced another cultural shock for me as I was selected to become one of the first black students to integrate our local junior high school. There were nine of us who moved into an all-white school of about 1,000 students. I didn't want to leave my haven, nor did I want to leave my all-black school environment, which had become my home. But my family told me the integration movement was necessary for our community and me.

It was a tough, emotional year for the few black students attending the school as we had to endure some challenging situations. During that school year, I realized that white students were no smarter or better than the black students, which greatly prepared me for my future years in adulthood.

Sometime around my 16th birthday in 1966, after I got my driver's license, I remember our racial name had changed officially from "Negro" to "black." In just 16 years, I had three different legal racial designations from the United States government (colored, Negro and black).

My childhood years in the 1960s were a transformative time in U.S. history — the civil rights movement; the assassinations of John F. Kennedy, the Rev. Dr. Martin Luther King Jr., Malcolm X and Robert Kennedy; the Vietnam War; the Black Panther Party; and the hippie-flower power movement.

However, throughout the 1960s and later, the pictures of those white-based biblical characters never changed. Those white biblical characters remained embedded in our church Bibles and also entrenched in our minds.

## Off to College

My next cultural milestone involved attending North Carolina A&T State University in Greensboro, North Carolina, a historically black university. I enrolled in the fall of 1968, about six months after the assassination of civil rights icon the Rev. Dr. Martin Luther King Jr.

By the time I entered college in 1968, my racial identity was black as the term "Negro" slowly phased out. I liked the name "black" and the racial self-esteem boost that went along with the word. I remember my beginnings at A&T — legendary soul singer James Brown had released a song that became our anthem, "Say It Loud — I'm Black and I'm Proud."

A&T was a cultural blessing for me. The late 1960s and 1970s was an explosion for the rebirth and expansion of black history and culture, which created a connection to African traditions and customs.

I found myself immersed within a society of students from across the United States and some foreign countries. Students with different ideas and new backgrounds enlightened me on news, events and stories about the black race.

I remember students who came from the northeastern cities telling me about Marcus Garvey, Langston Hughes, The Last Poets and other black luminaries. I remember the northern students wearing clothing with the symbolic colors of red, black and green — associated with the Pan-African colors of the blood of African ancestry (red), the people (black) and the land of Africa (green).

Part of my memorable and best experiences was pledging and joining the Iota Phi Theta Fraternity in the fall of 1969. The brotherhood connections and longtime friends are treasures of a lifetime.

I remember prominent black lecturers speaking on campus, including Stokley Carmichael (Kwame Ture) and Dick Gregory. The list of dynamic lecturers and speakers that visited our campus triggered thoughts and dreams about my own upcoming future of African research.

The college experiences provided the basic platform for me to begin exploring African history for the next 45 years — and I never stopped. I will always be indebted to my alma mater for the things I learned, absorbed, failed and achieved during my undergraduate years.

## California Dreaming

I graduated from college in May 1973, and that summer I embarked on my next cultural milestone. I left my comfortable surroundings in North Carolina and moved to Inglewood, California. Yes, Los Angeles County, home to L.A., Hollywood, Beverly Hills, Long Beach, Compton and so many dynamic cities. A county of more than 7 million people brimming with diversity and multicultural experiences. There were people from all over the world, working and living together.

Moving to the Los Angeles area changed my ideas and perceptions. I landed a job in accounting with an international restaurant company. Just within my department of about 40 people, I had co-workers from the United Kingdom, Armenia, the Philippines, Thailand, Australia, Egypt, South America and Mexico.

I worked there for 5½ years, made a lot of good friends and learned fascinating things about other countries and cultures. I began to ask general questions on topics such as:

- What religion are you and tell me about it?
- Were there any black people living in your areas when you were growing up?
- Why do you talk about your country and culture with such great pride (because I was envious and wanted to do the same with my limited cultural knowledge)?
- Have you ever traveled to the southeastern United States, where there is a lot more visible racism?
- What are your views on black people in the United States?

Living on the West Coast made me realize there was a vast big world full of people from different backgrounds and beliefs. The people I met were proud of their historical identities. I began to think that I wanted to talk about my race with more purpose and positiveness. I continued to listen, observe and read about the history of the black race when small opportunities occurred.

I was still in my 20s, so research and study had to fit into my fun-filled California lifestyle, but I managed to show discipline by reading often.

## Treasures in a Bookstore

I moved from California back to North Carolina in March 1978, landing a job in Charlotte, North Carolina, working for a growing southern regional bank. It was a big bank full of good people, but not nearly the cultural diversity I experienced in California.

My next significant cultural advancement didn't involve the bank but came from a black-owned bookstore that I found in Charlotte called The Undercover Book Source. The owner was a strong and vibrant young woman from the Tidewater/Hampton, Virginia, area named Angela Simpson.

The Undercover Book Source was a well-stocked book store with literary materials from some of the best-known authors on African/ black history and other culturally related topics. The inventory of materials was broad, expansive and covered authors and subjects of which I had never heard.

I visited the store often to purchase books and materials. Angela and I discussed my mission of historical research and she provided overviews and synopsis on books that matched my interests.

She also highlighted new books to expand my research, and this whole process delighted me. Angela had an unlimited selection of books that satisfied my curiosity, which expanded to poetry, the Harlem Renaissance and other topics. She is the person that introduced me to authors on the African history experience, such as J.A. Rogers, Drusilla Dunjee Houston, Chancellor Williams, Claude McKay, Paul L. Dunbar, Ivan Van Sertima and William Hansberry.

My monthly book purchases grew rapidly during the 1980s until I had an extensive personal library of quality materials. This bookstore led me to grow culturally and mentally. I read each book from cover to cover, hoping to find gold nuggets of information that would enlighten and direct me to explore new authors and material.

I pursued various authors with differing styles and sifted through volumes of material. I included both black and white authors in my historical readings and research. As a researcher, I learned you couldn't agree with all writers on every subject. You learn to read, compare, disagree and filter information until you attain your level of understanding.

It's hard to find one author that can satisfy all research needs, so it's better to research and grow continuously.

## The Lecture Circuit

During the 1980s and 1990s, I developed a passion for lecturing, where I consistently spoke about the importance of African history. This mission to educate people took me to public schools, churches, universities and community events. I spoke in more than 100 different public schools, which allowed me to be recognized as the winner of the prestigious First Union National Bank Volunteer in Education Award in 1992.

The second highlight of this time in my life was a two-year engagement as a regular lecturer at the Afro-American Cultural Center in Charlotte from 1991 to 1992. It was here that I developed some of my memorable lecture materials, which included "Black People in The Bible," "The Legendary Ethiopians," "Black Cowboys" and "African Travelers to the New World, Before Columbus."

Lecturing required that I always researched and strengthened my knowledge of subject matter materials from a wide range of sources.

## Travels to Africa

My cultural journey was enhanced by two educational trips to Africa in the 1990s. I needed to touch the soil, walk among the people and inhale the air of this great continent.

One trip was to the West African countries of Senegal and The Gambia. My goal was to absorb the slave trade process and just to be in the motherland. A second trip was to Egypt, where I wanted to witness the splendors of this great nation and confirm my thoughts that the original Egyptians were from the black nations of people.

These two trips made lasting impressions and served as cultural bridges to confirm my dedication to revealing more truth about the wonderful African people.

All of these points were building blocks on my journey, culminating in my writing books on the Ethiopian Queen Makeda (the Queen of Sheba) and now this very special book, "Children of Genesis." Years of diligence, preparation and research led me to fulfill this sense of purpose for humanity — to educate, process, debate and form better understandings of the history of Africa.

## Moving into the 21st Century

Within the 21st century, my expertise has centered around ancient history, the B.C. (Before Christ) era. While many people find ancient history "too old, tedious and boring," I find it wonderful and exhilarating because these were the times when black nations led the world in terms of great civilizations.

The black nations were at the very beginnings of ancient world advancement and were at the forefront of progress. They led the way by inventing and creating paths for ancient humanity to move forward systematically through these periods. Sometimes I feel like I can just reach out and almost touch the characters as they marched through the pages of ancient times. Mentally, I can see them in pictures and scenes of great stories as they led humanity.

I wake up each day with a passion for seeking new information to grow and acquire new paths of knowledge. *It's a burning desire fueled by a flame that never grows dim.* I continuously need to explore and gain a comprehensive understanding of African-based people.

## Why This Book

I feel that I was destined to write this book, and I realize the preparation process started a long time ago. The actual realization started about five years ago. I began to feel something, an urge or inner voice, to create a long-lasting and impactful book.

Initially, I ignored the instinctive feelings for about a year, thinking the desire simply would go away.

The original handwritten draft started in 2017 and has undergone multiple edits and updates as I worked alongside my editor in crafting the manuscript. From the very beginning, I constantly prayed to God just to walk with me and guide me towards a final work that would be pleasing in His sight.

And through the pages of my life's journey, I present this book as an effort to keep the eternal flame burning on the splendors and wonders of the ancient black nations and empires.

# Reader's Guide

People tend to think ancient history is an uninteresting subject — something that is very old, too abstract, tedious or even dull. "It's so long ago, too far back to even think about it," is the feedback I have heard when giving lectures. Here are some thoughts that may aid you in understanding the structure and intent of this book:

**1.) The goal of this book is to create greater awareness of the ethnic representation of the people in the Old Testament.** This book is about historical subjects and will not concentrate on religion. I respectfully leave the religious coverage to the trained men and women. It may appear that occasionally I venture over the religious line when presenting certain historical subjects as it is almost impossible to separate all the religious concepts from historical events — but that was certainly my goal.

**2.) The scope of this book covers the Old Testament, which occurred before the birth of Christ.** I will identify biblical information that includes black nations that existed during that era. These black nations went back to 5000 B.C. and were much older than Abraham and the authors of the Old Testament. My goal is to enlighten and educate the world about the ancient black nations and people contained in the Old Testament. I want to create more dialogue and critical thinking on Old Testament characters and information.

**3.) It is not my desire to disrespect any nation or race of people during this book.** No racial insults, no human degrading are necessary to present my information. However, there will be times when I am bold and direct on certain subjects because courage is required when dealing with ancient history and civilization. I believe people can navigate the course of truthful accounts that will enhance the overall landscape for a better understanding of humanity. I appeal to the intellect, logic and rational places in both our hearts and minds as we embark on this journey.

**4.) There will be times when I aggressively reclaim black nations' rightful place in the Old Testament.** Within this book, I strategically seize opportunities to uplift the black nations and people as they march across the pages of the scriptures. Ancient civilizations involve stories and events from so long ago that it is almost impossible to write a 100 percent generally accepted book.

There will be isolated concepts or dates that are debatable from varying sources. In reading this book, I encourage readers to take the areas of debate and create levels of intellectual exploration and advancement so the world can be further enlightened on the contributions of ancient black nations. Humanity thrives best when full information is available and accessible for all people.

**5.) The scope of this book will NOT include debates on the Bible's authenticity.** There may be readers wanting to debate the Bible's accuracy, the origin of its information and the identity of the authors. I fully recognize these topics, but they are not part of the specific scope of this book. Within my scope, I took the King James Version of the Old Testament in its written format. I did not add or take away from the actual written text. I used the actual scriptures and verses to guide my identification of the biblical black nations and their people.

**6.) Independent of the Bible, ancient writers and other historians knew black nations existed in the Old Testament era.** The additional supplemental information I inserted in this book was to demonstrate that external historians, archaeologist and scholars also were aware of these ancient black nations with their research that was independent of the Bible. Their historical research and conclusions run parallel and in general agreement with the historical information contained in the Old Testament.

**7.) My goal was to use the terms "Hebrew" and "Israelite" in their correct places within this book.** Sometimes it became challenging and if I made any mistakes, I sincerely apologize from my heart.

**8.) A decision was made to not include every Bible verse on the stories contained in this book.** Selected verses were sometimes used along with summaries of stories and the listing of biblical references where information can be located in the Old Testament.

**9.) Finally, this book will not include the New Testament.** The timelines between the Old Testament and New Testament involve different populations of people that changed dramatically over hundreds of years. With the emergence of the Greeks and Romans in the New Testament, the ethnic makeup of characters is different.

As an ancient civilization historian, my focus remains with the black nations in the Old Testament.

Peace be unto everyone,

**Ronald Harrill**

# Prologue

*"One of the most popular reasons people study the Bible is to learn about the historical events it records. So much of the Bible is devoted to history."*

**Robert H. Stein**[1]

For the past 500 years, the identities of powerful black nations have remained hidden among the pages of the Bible's Old Testament. These black nations led the ancient world towards civilization, invented writing, erected phenomenal monuments, and built canal systems to manage large rivers. Yet, each of these empires' identities was hijacked and reinterpreted by the modern world for social conveniences. These nations continue to suffer from identity theft crisis. Misleading representations of their people are commonplace in pictures, movies, paintings, social media and books.

Looking at the Bible using historical lenses instead of the traditional religious filters, this book takes a wide-angle view of the people, places, and events from the Old Testament era. When analyzing the Old Testament and reviewing people from a historical perspective, several questions surface:

- Who were the people living during the Old Testament era?
- What lifestyles did the people maintain during this period?
- Were the people part of a progressive civilization?
- Were the Hebrews/Israelites leaders in ancient civilization?

1 Brand, Chad; Draper, Charles; England, Archie (2003). Holman Illustrated Bible Dictionary. Nashville, TN: Holman Bible Publishers. Page 207.

The Book of Genesis tells the story of Noah and the Great Flood that destroyed all known human life, except for Noah's family. Chapters 9 and 10 identified Noah's three sons who had the task of repopulating the earth after the Great Flood through their descendants:

> *"And the sons of Noah, that went forth of the ark, were Shem, and Ham, and Japheth: and Ham is the father of Canaan."*
>
> **Genesis 9:18**

> *"Now these are the generations of the sons of Noah, Shem, Ham, and Japheth: and unto them were sons born after the flood."*
>
> **Genesis 10:1**

The Holman Illustrated Bible Dictionary provides additional information on Noah's sons (see chart):

- **Shem:** Considered the father of Asiatic nations of people, including the Israelites, Moabites, Assyrians and Persians. They are called the Semite people ("Noah's oldest son and original ancestor of Semitic peoples including Israel");[2]
- **Ham:** Considered the father of African-descent nations of people, such as the Egyptians, Ethiopians, Canaanites and Sidonians. They are called the Hamite people. ("Second of Noah's three sons. Ham became the original ancestor of the Cushites, the Egyptians and the Canaanites");[3]
- **Japheth:** Considered the father of Indo- European nations of people, such as the Romans and Greeks. They are called the Japhetite people ("One of Noah's three sons, either the youngest or next to youngest. These names point to Japheth as having been the progenitor of the Indo-European peoples who lived to the north and west of Israel, farthest from Israel)."[4]

---

2 Brand, Chad; Draper, Charles; England, Archie (2003). Holman Illustrated Bible Dictionary. Nashville, TN.: Holman Bible Publishers. Page 1481.

3 Ibid., Page 706.

4 Ibid., Page 870.

# FAMILY TREE

*Genealogical table of Noah's descendants*

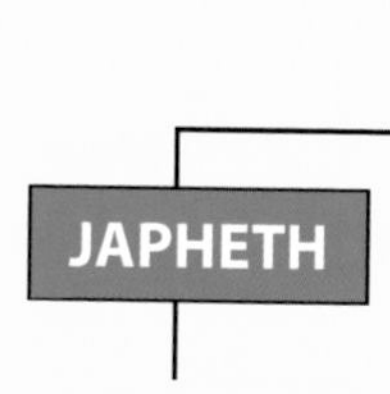

**NOAH**

## JAPHETH

Gomer, Magog, Madai, Javan, Tubal, Meshech, Tiras

**Sons of Gomer**
Ashkenaz, Riphath, Togarmah

**Sons of Javan**
Elishah, Tarshish, Kittim, Dodanim

## HAM

Cush, Mizriam, Canaan, Phut

**Sons of Cush**
Nimrod, Seba, Havilah, Sabtah, Sabtechah, Ramah

**Sons of Ramah**
Sheba, Dedan

**Sons of Mizriam**
Ludim, Anamin, Lehabim, Napthtuhim, Pathrusim, Capthorim, Casluhim

**Son of Casluhim**
Philistim

**Sons of Canaan**
Sidon, Heth, Jebusite, Amorite, Girgashite, Hivite, Arkite, Sinite, Arvadite, Zemarite, Hamathite

## SHEM

Arxphaxad, Aram, Elam, Asshur, Lud

**Son of Arxphaxad**
Salah

**Son of Salah**
Eber

**Sons of Eber**
Joktan, Peleg

**Sons of Joktan**
Amodad, Sheleph, Hazarmaveth, Jerah, Hadoram, Uza, Dikhah, Obal, Abimael, Sheba, Ophir, Jobab, Havilah

**Descendants of Peleg**
Reu, Serug, Terah, Abram

**Sons of Aram**
Hul, Gether, Meshec, Uz

The following verses instructed Noah's sons on the task of repopulating the earth:

> *"And God blessed Noah and his sons, and said unto them, 'Be fruitful, and multiply, and replenish the earth.'"*
>
> **Genesis 9:1**

> *"And you, be ye fruitful, and multiply; bring forth abundantly in the earth, and multiply therein."*
>
> **Genesis 9:7**

Genesis 10 details the plans for the repopulation of the earth and the role of Noah's three sons. Each son was responsible for creating his ancestral bloodlines that would result in his descendants founding designated nations of people for the earth.

Genesis 10 contains the 30 genealogy verses that recorded the descendants of each of Noah's sons. Within these verses lies the authentic Old Testament nations' birth records tied to Noah's sons. Genesis 10 is the biblical source that supports the beginnings of the 70 known nations that descended from Noah's three sons (sometimes called the Table of Nations).

The Table of Nations reveals:

- Ham and his descendants had 30 nations (43 percent of the nations).
- Shem and his descendants had 26 nations (37 percent of the nations).
- Japheth and his descendants had 14 nations (20 percent of the nations).

Additionally, Ham's family tree appears in 15 verses, or 50 percent of the 30 verses (Genesis 10: 6-20). Shem's family tree appears in 11 verses, or 37 percent (Genesis 10: 21-31). Japheth's family tree appears in only four verses (Genesis 10: 2-5), or 13 percent.

To put this information into context, Ham and his descendants received nearly four times more genealogical verses than Japheth and his descendants. Ham also received more verses than Shem even though the Old Testament's main characters, the Israelites, are Shem's descendants. Moreover, Ham and his descendants had the same number of biblical verses (15) as the descendants of Shem and Japheth combined (15).

## CHALLENGING QUESTION

If the black nations are dominant in Genesis 10 and the Table of Nations, how did they disappear in modern-day representations of the Old Testament?

The Old Testament centers around nations of people, which was a way of grouping people during that era. Old Testament writers did not know about terms such as race and racial identification. The racial classifications of people along color lines and ethnic origins were a European-related invention created approximately in the 15th and 16th centuries.

Within this book, there will be an ongoing comparison between Old Testament writings on ancient black nations and the following additional sources that exist on ancient black nations:

- Inscriptions and carvings left on ancient monuments and statues.
- Excavations and archaeological findings from old biblical countries.
- Historians and writers' reports who lived in the late B.C. and early A.D. periods.

- Early Greek writings from the B.C. and early A.D. periods.
- Writers and historians from the 18th to 20th centuries.

From these detailed comparisons, two crucial questions arose with corresponding answers:

- Did the Old Testament books and the above-referenced sources talk about the existence of prominent and influential black nations during ancient civilization? **Yes**, they did.
- Did the Old Testament and the above-referenced sources talk about black nations being part of the beginnings and critical contributors to early civilization? That's a resounding **Yes**.

The Old Testament is such a rich depository of information on ancient black nations. Using the Bible as a history book may seem uncomfortable, but it is full of information on these nations. The Bible authenticates the existence of ancient black societies by recording a strong presence of Hamite history and their importance.

The black nations never left the books of the Old Testament; modern humanity merely decided to provide a remake of characters and societies for their self-interests. Modern theories and assumptions about the identity of Old Testament nations regularly contradict how Old Testament writers depicted these nations.

## A Wide-Angle Historical View

When the early Hebrews arrived on the historical scene, the Hamite nations were already leading the ancient world. The Hamites already had built major cities, established regional political relationships and created strong commercial trade between the quadrant of black nations — Egypt, Ethiopia, early Canaan and early Mesopotamia (Babylon).

Egypt was leading the world in science, medicine, architecture and had already built the world's iconic pyramids. The Sphinx had been built in Egypt during an age so long ago that historians cannot calculate its creation date. The Sphinx represents an incredibly old Hamite nation and the face on this eternal statue is clearly that of a black man.

Before the Hebrews' existence, the early Babylonians, Ethiopians and Egyptians maintained urban living areas, farmed their lands and domesticated the animals. They managed the Nile, Tigris and Euphrates rivers during droughts and overflowing annual cycles. They skillfully built dams, canals, irrigation systems and constructed massive lakes-reservoirs to store water during drought periods.

During the Old Testament era, the Hebrews/Israelites were not major inventors. A lot of the inventions from that era came from the Hamite nations. For example, the Sumerians in Mesopotamia and the Egyptians were leaders in the early development of writing and monument building.

When the Israelites migrated into the Canaan lands, they moved into cities the Canaanites had already built. Moreover, the historical Canaanites were not the stereotyped people portrayed in modern times. The Israelites never eliminated the Canaanites during the Old Testament days and, in fact, lived among the Canaanites.

The Semites, including the Israelites, were slower than the Hamites in learning how to work with iron and metal workings. Examples of Hamite metal usage would be the early Hittites (the descendants of Ham's son, Canaan), who were among the first known biblical groups to work with iron. The Canaanites and Egyptians possessed metal-laden chariots centuries before the Israelites, who later acquired these military items during King David's lifetime.

The Old Testament is primarily about two ethnic nations: the Semites as the stars and leading characters (the protagonists) and the Hamites as supporting characters, occasional allies and frequent adversaries (the antagonists). This book's goal is to showcase the ancient black nations for the world to appreciate and better understand their phenomenal achievements, as they built the foundations of civilization that we continue to use today.

While the Hebrews authored the Old Testament, they did not author the overall book of ancient civilization and history. At the same time, the world should be grateful for the Hebrew writers for creating the Old Testament and its place in world culture.

Ultimately, the purpose of this book is for readers to grow in the following areas:

- Increased learning and appreciation of diversity among people.
- Expanded knowledge through appreciation of the biblical characters.
- Increased learning about ancient civilizations.
- Greater awareness and appreciation for Africa and its history.
- A better understanding of world cultures and customs.

God knows the deepest part of my heart, my strong humanitarian feelings and my desire to have wisdom, knowledge and understanding for the completion of this book. I pray that my thoughts and actions will not offend other humans, races and groups of people. However, a book like this requires cultural courage and fortitude to complete the mission.

Peace be unto everyone,

**Ronald Harrill**

# Hamite Lands

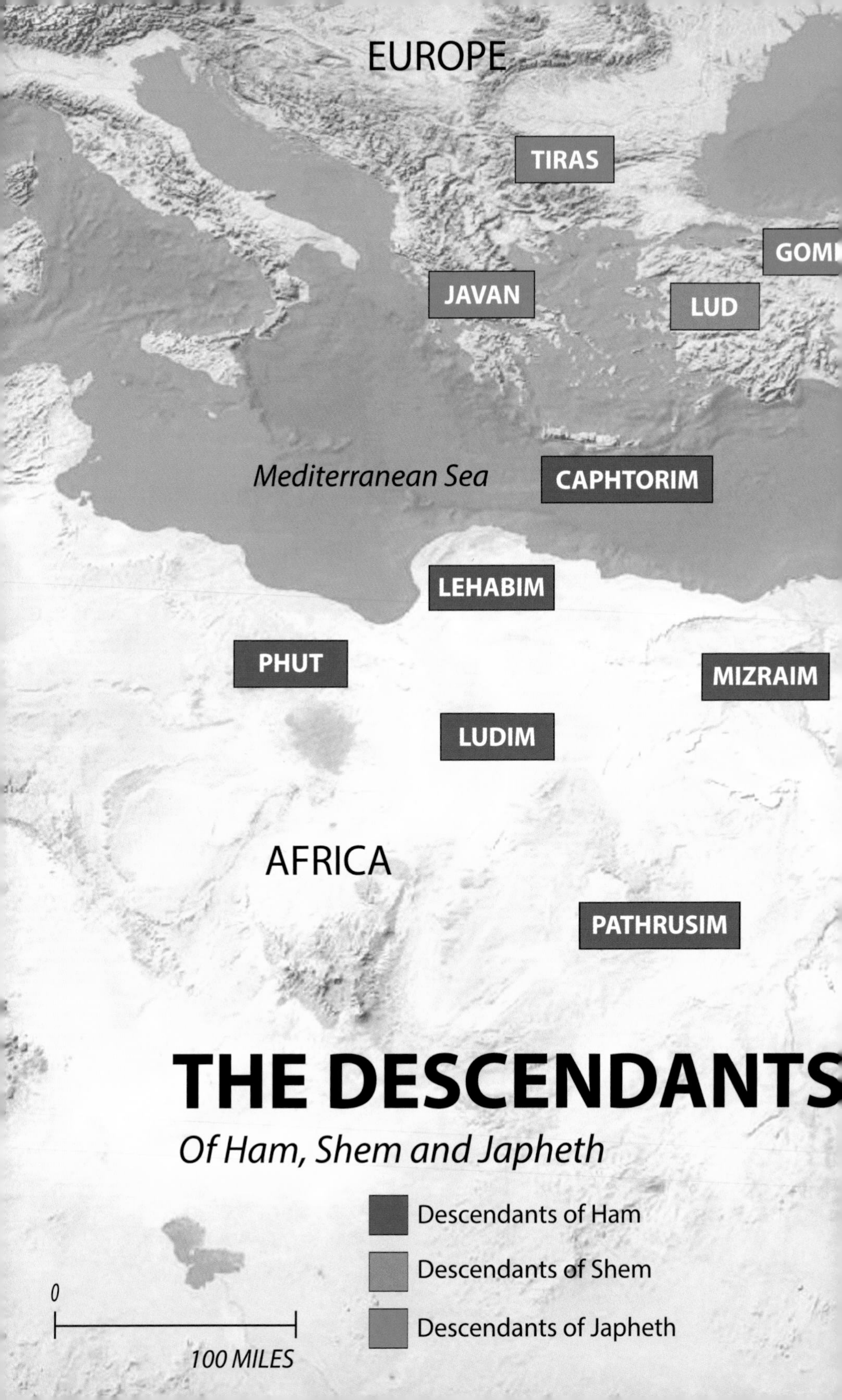
EUROPE
TIRAS
GOM
JAVAN
LUD
Mediterranean Sea
CAPHTORIM
LEHABIM
PHUT
MIZRAIM
LUDIM
AFRICA
PATHRUSIM
THE DESCENDANTS
Of Ham, Shem and Japheth
Descendants of Ham
Descendants of Shem
Descendants of Japheth
0
100 MILES

ASHKENAZ
MAGOG
Black Sea
MESHECH
TUBAL
TOGARMAH
ASHKENAZ
Caspian Sea
ASSHUR
HETH
MADAI
ASIA
ARAM
NIMROD
CANAAN
ELAM
MASH
ARPHAXAD
DEDAN
HAVILAH
Persian Gulf
RAMAH
ARABIA
SHEBA
Red Sea
JOKTAN
HAVILAH
RAMAH
UZAL
HAZARMAVETH
SHEBA
USH
OPHIR
Arabian Sea

# 1

# In the Beginning

*"There are a people, now forgotten, discovered, while others were yet barbarians, the elements of the arts and sciences. A race of men, now rejected from society for their sable skin and frizzled hair, founded on the study of laws of nature, those civil and religious systems which still govern today."*

**Count C.F. Volney, 1793[5]**

## OBJECTIVE

This opening chapter will discuss the Hamite nations and people that were part of the repopulation of the earth after the Great Flood. Ham's descendants were among the most documented nations, which include the Ethiopians, Egyptians, Canaanites and early Babylonians.

The Old Testament provides historical insight into the biblical era civilizations and the people that lived during that timeline. This chapter will focus primarily on Ham and the Hamite black nations. During the Old Testament days, people were classified by "nations of people." The general definition of a nation in biblical terms was a grouping of related people.

This basic grouping structure started with **individuals** who formed **families,** who consolidated their kinship organizations into **clans**

5. Supreme Understanding (2013). "When the World Was Black— The Untold History of the World's First Civilizations." Atlanta, GA: Supreme Design Publishing. Page 19.

of people. Subgroups of the clans then formed a higher level called **tribes** and the collective bonded tribes of people would form **nations**.

For example, the 12 Tribes of Israel started with the sons of Jacob (individuals). Each son's families clustered into clans, which moved into a tribe. Thus, there were 12 tribes because each son had a tribe.

When all the tribes came together, they formed a nation. This book will adhere to the Old Testament classifications of people as nations, not by races. The terms "black nations," "white nations" and "Asiatic nations" will be used to provide context.

## Profile: Ham

The descendants of Noah's son Ham were the most documented group of nations in Genesis 10. Within Genesis 10: 2-31 for the earth's repopulation after the Great Flood, Ham's descendants had the most number of listed nations. They built more cities than the other sons of Noah and their individual stories included two dynamic Hamite descendants, Canaan and Nimrod.

Genesis 10: 6-20 covers the genealogy of Ham and his descendants. Additional highlights of these verses include:

- Ham's descendants lived in Africa, Asia, Arabia and the Mediterranean islands. It is important to note that the Hamite nations were not just in African lands; they were associated with conquering and expansion.
- Ham's son Canaan (Genesis 10:15-19) and Ham's grandson Nimrod (Genesis 10:8-12) received special genealogy recognition and significant achievements.
- Nimrod is credited as the founder of Mesopotamia, which included Babylon. In Genesis 10:10 covering Nimrod, "Shinar" is mentioned. "Shinar" is the old Hebrew word for the region known as Mesopotamia.
- Canaan is credited as the ancestor of the many groups that occupied ancient Canaan lands.

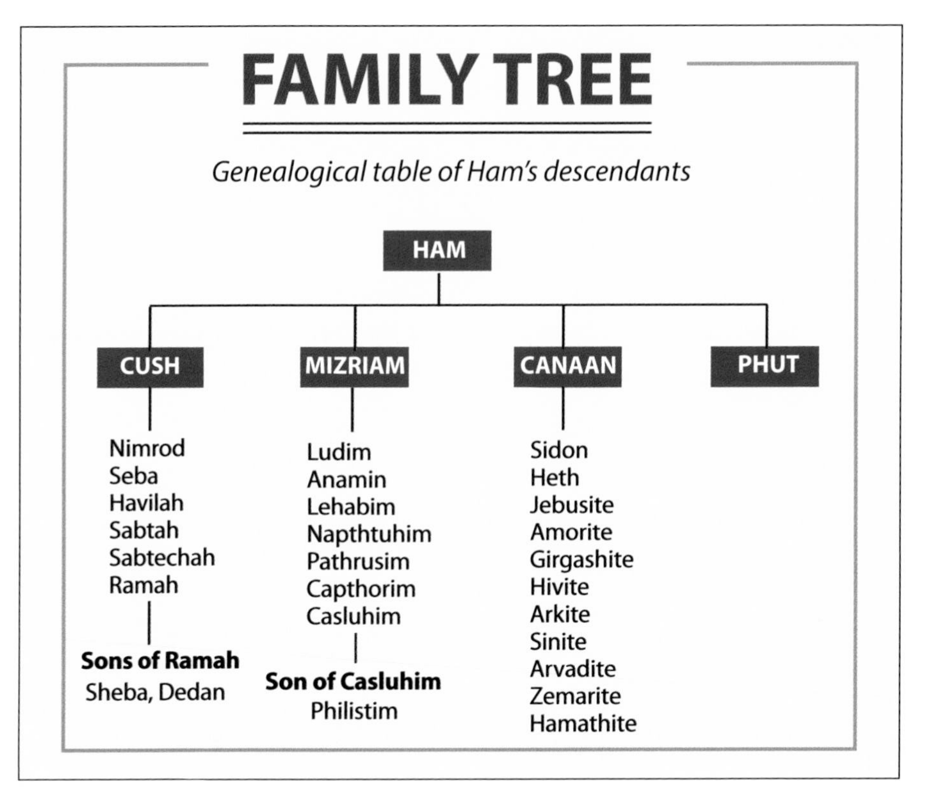


- Nimrod and Canaan each received more genealogy verses and recognition than Noah's son Japheth, the father of the white nations.
- "Mizraim" is an ancient Hebrew word for "Egypt." Ham's son, Mizraim, was the biblical ancestor for the Egyptian people (Genesis 10:13-14).
- Ham's son Cush is the ancestor of the legendary Cushite (Ethiopian) empire (Genesis 10:6-8).

The Israelites were the main characters of the Old Testament and the Hamites were the lead supporting characters. Without the multitude of Ham's descendants, many Old Testament stories would be incomplete. Hamite nations participated throughout the books and chapters of Old Testament literature. Ham's descendants included:

| Ethiopians | Egyptians | Canaanites | Babylonians |
|---|---|---|---|
| Sidonians* | Amorites* | Hittites* | Jebusites* |
| Girgasites * | Hivites * | Philistines * | Phoenicians * |

* These groups were descendants of Canaan's sons, Sidon and Heth.

## The Hamite Presence

Here is a summary of Old Testament references to the Hamite people:

- Egypt is listed in the Old Testament more than 500 times.
- Canaan and the Canaanites are listed in the Old Testament more than 150 times.
- Cush /Ethiopia is listed in the Old Testament more than 50 times.
- Babylon is listed in the Old Testament more than 200 times.
- Chaldea is listed in the Old Testament more than 70 times.
- The Hittites are listed in the Old Testament more than 40 times.

These nations were initially Hamite nations, but later some nations were invaded and blended with Semites. The original Hamites did not leave their lands during the B.C. era invasions and migrations.

Collectively, there are more than 1,000 biblical references of Ham's family tree in the Old Testament. This number does not include all descendants of Cush, Canaan and Mizraim, such as the Phoenicians and the Sidonians, which would increase the reference count.

## The Curse of Ham

"The Curse of Ham" is a modern religious interpretation of the Genesis 9 story involving the supposed curse placed on Ham by his father, Noah. The story involves Ham telling his brothers that he observed their father in a drunk and naked condition. As a result, Noah placed a curse on his grandson, Canaan (see Genesis 9:20-27):

> *"And he said, Cursed be Canaan; a servant of servants shall he be unto his brethren."*
>
> **Genesis 9:25**

This curse was a misinterpretation, implying the descendants of Ham (the black nations) would become subordinate to and servants for the nations of people fathered by Noah's other two sons, Shem and Japheth.

There was no biblical curse on Ham to substantiate the theory on the subordination of Ham and his other three sons, meaning that only one son, Canaan, and his people (the Canaanites) were subject to Noah's curse.

The Abrahamic religions (Judaism, Christianity and Islam) expanded on this biblical story to imply there was a curse on Ham and all of his sons — meaning the entire black race was cursed to become servants to the descendants of Shem and Japheth.

This misguided interpretation was used for centuries to support the subordination, oppression and enslavement of African/black people. This subject was discussed and supported by religious institutions for centuries.

Even though these religious groups' rationale and interpretation were erroneous, they did recognize Ham as the father of Africans and the black nations. The purpose of this story was to show the acknowledgment and support of Ham's identity as the ancestral father of the black nations.

## Scholarly Citations

Scholars and researchers have long studied the story of Noah and his sons. Flavius Josephus was a noted and respected first-century Jewish-Roman historian who recorded Jewish history. In his research, Josephus interpreted Ham's descendants as having populated Africa and adjoining parts of Asia.[6]

Another reference that supports the ethnic distinction for Noah's three sons comes from French professor scholar Charles Seignobos (1854-1942) in his writings on the Egyptians and Chaldeans, members of the Hamite-black nations:

> *"It is within the limits of Asia and Africa that the first civilized people developed. The Egyptians in the Nile valley; and the Chaldeans in the plains of the Euphrates (Mesopotamia region). These were people of sedentary and peaceful pursuits. Their skin was dark, hair short and thick, the lips strong."*[7]

F.C. Gilbert (1867-1947), a noted Jewish scholar, wrote the following:

> *"Without a doubt, the Hamites, the early Egyptian people, had the most ancient records."*[8]

19th-century British scholar and historian George Rawlinson cited in his book "Ancient Monarchies, Vol. 1:"

> *"For the last three thousand years, the world has been mainly indebted to the Semitic and Indo-European races for its advancement, but it was otherwise in the first ages. Egypt, Babylon, Mizraim and Nimrod, both descendants of Ham, led the way and acted as pioneers of mankind in the various untrodden fields of art, science and literature. Alphabet writings, astronomy, history, chronology, architecture, plastic art, sculpture, navigation, agriculture and textile industries seem to have had their origin in one or the other of these countries."*[9]

---

6. Josephus, Flavius; Whiston, William (translator); Boer, Paul A. (editor) (2014). The Antiquities of the Jews: Volume I (Books I - X). Scotts Valley, CA: CreateSpace Independent Publishing Platform. Page 46.
7. The Holy Bible, Black Heritage Edition: King James Version (1976). Nashville, TN: Today, Inc. Page 79.
8. Ibid., Page 80.
9. Houston, Drusilla Dunjee (1985). Wonderful Ethiopians of the Ancient Cushite Empire. Baltimore, MD: Black Classics Press. Page 18.

Christian Charles Josias von Bunsen (1791-1860), a 19th-century German scholar says in his book "Philosophy of Ancient History:"

> *"The Hamitic family, as Rawlinson proves must be given the credit for being the fountainhead of civilization. This family comprised the ancient Ethiopians, the Egyptians, the original Canaanites and the old Chaldeans. The inscriptions of the Chaldean monuments prove their race affinity. The Bible proves their relationship. It names the sons of Ham as Cush, Mizraim, Phut and the race of Canaan. Mizraim peopled Egypt and Canaan, the land later possessed by the Hebrews. Phut located in Africa and Cush extended his colonies over a wide domain."*[10]

These respected scholars and historians supported the biblical heritage of Noah's son Ham and his descendants as being members of the ancient black nations — a viewpoint that dates back hundreds of years.

## Historical Timeline

In the modern era, there have been approximately 2,000 years of history since the birth of Christ. However, in the B.C. era before Christ, there are more than 4,000 years of history for some biblical black nations such as Ethiopia, Egypt and the Mesopotamian region. The ancient history B.C. era timeline is twice as long as the modern era timeline. Moreover, Ethiopian history goes back to 5000 B.C. and beyond.

Semite people were living in Mesopotamia during its early stages, but they were not the original developers of Mesopotamian civilization. Developed Semite nations began to appear around 2500 B.C., but are not as old as the Hamite nations. Semites initially appeared in Canaan lands during the Early Bronze Age (2200–2000 B.C.).

Steve Wyrick, a professor of religion at the University of Mary Hardin-Baylor, states "the place of origin for the Semites is difficult to determine."[11]

10. Houston, Drusilla Dunjee (1985). Wonderful Ethiopians of the Ancient Cushite Empire. Baltimore, MD: Black Classics Press. Page 19.
11. Brand, Chad; Draper, Charles; England, Archie (2003). Holman Illustrated Bible Dictionary. Nashville, TN.: Holman Bible Publishers. Page 1461.

Another Semite empire, the Assyrian Empire, only goes back to about 1500-1300 B.C. In contrast, Hamite nations existed more than 1,000 years before Abraham's birth. Historians estimate the Egyptians built the pyramids around 2500 B.C., some 1,000 years before Isaac, Jacob, Joseph and Moses lived.

Israelite interaction with Hamite nations such as Ethiopia, Canaan and Egypt was common throughout the Old Testament, usually in the areas of economic trade, military battles, government and politics. There was minimal Israelite interaction with Greece, Rome and other white nations in the Old Testament.

Moreover, the descendants of Noah's son Japheth — the white nations — received little mention within the first five books of the Old Testament. Genesis, Exodus, Leviticus, Numbers and Deuteronomy concentrate on stories involving Shem and Ham and their descendants.

The rise of Greece and Rome marked the beginnings of civilized white nations in the biblical era. Since the emergence of Greece around 950 B.C. and Rome near 750 B.C., the European nations and people have been a strong, visible and high-achieving civilization in world leadership for the past 3,000 years.

White nations are very visible, noteworthy and prominent in the New Testament stories and events. However, ancient history records before 1000 B.C. show little recorded information of white nations significantly participating in the Old Testament (see chart, next page).

The first prominent and visible nation listed on this chart and also first listed in the Old Testament was Ethiopia, as referenced in the following passage from the second chapter of Genesis:

> *"And the name of the second river is Gihon: the same is it that compasseth the whole land of Ethiopia."*
>
> **Genesis 2:13**

The European countries of Greece and Rome are listed last on the chart in terms of civilization, as the white nations emerged after the Hamite and Semite nations.

# TIMELINE

*History of ancient biblical civilizations*

Descendants of Ham
Descendants of Shem
Descendants of Japheth

**5000 B.C.**
Ancient Cush (Ethiopia) and Mesopotamia

**4000 B.C.**
Babylon (Mesopotamian city)

**4000 B.C.**
Egypt (unified in 3300 B.C.)

**4000-3000 B.C.**
Canaan (original Canaanites)

**2500 B.C.**
Great Pyramids built

**1900 B.C.**
Abraham's life

**1750 B.C.**
Minoan people

**1700 B.C.**
Israelites captive in Egypt

**1400 B.C.**
Assyrians rise

**1300 B.C.**
Moses' death

**970 B.C.**
David's death

**950 B.C.**
Greek civilization

**750 B.C.**
Rome civilization

The chart shows the approximate beginning dates for civilization in the prominent biblical era countries. This chart is in alignment with the slow start given to the white nations in Genesis 10 for the repopulation of the earth.

This timeline also supports the Table of Nations, where the white nations (Japheth's descendants) received the lowest allocated number of nations in the Old Testament. Noah's son Japheth only received 14 of the 70 nations (20 percent), which was the lowest number among the three sons.

To add more perspective to the timeline:

- Abraham lived almost 1,000 years before Greek civilization was prominent.
- Isaac, Jacob, Judah and Joseph all lived and died before Greece and Rome civilizations.
- The Great Pyramid was approximately 1,500 years older than Greek civilization.
- There is little evidence showing that prominent biblical characters Moses, David and Solomon interacted much with white nations.

## Changing Landscapes

When looking at people in the Middle East today, it may be difficult to reconcile how people living in the area looked thousands of years ago. Modern-day people living in current lands do not always look like the indigenous people as landscapes of humanity can change over time.

The United States is a perfect example of such a change. In less than 400 years, based on invasions and constant migrations, the major inhabitants have changed from its original indigenous people, the Native Americans. Today's United States population is a multiracial society that looks drastically different, including people of European, African, Hispanic-Latino and Asian descent.

The same concept applies in Canada, South America, the Caribbean Islands and Australia, where the original inhabitants of their lands became displaced, removed or eliminated from their homelands, becoming the minority population in countries they once controlled.

During the ancient times of the Old Testament era, changes in human population and land occupancy occurred numerous times throughout history. Factors commonly contributing were military invasions and wars, human migration patterns, natural disasters such as floods, earthquakes, famines and droughts. Over centuries, these events significantly altered the landscape of how human populations looked over time.

Ancient black nations such as Egypt, Canaan and the early Mesopotamian region endured dramatic changes. For thousands of years, Egypt has undergone numerous migrations, conquerings, invasions and occupations by a host of countries that include the Ethiopians, Assyrians, Libyans, Persians, the Greeks under Alexander the Great, Hyksos, Arabs, Ottoman Turks and France under Napoleon.

Israel also underwent numerous migrations, conquering invasions and occupations over thousands of years that include the Assyrians, Babylonians, Persians, the Greeks under Alexander the Great, Romans, Byzantine, Arabs and the Ottoman Empire.

## Summary

In summary, ancient biblical countries were invaded, overrun and became the products of intermixing. So the people currently living in those lands today do not look like the people who lived in those lands thousands of years ago.

## TALKING POINTS

According to Genesis 10, Ham's family tree (the Hamites) were the leaders in the nations that were part of the repopulation of the earth after the Great Flood. Within the Table of 70 Nations, Ham received 30 nations, with Shem receiving 26 nations and Japheth receiving 14 nations. Ham's family tree contained some of the most dynamic, vibrant nations in the Old Testament — such as the Egyptians, Ethiopians, ancient Babylonians, Chaldeans, Canaanites, Hittites, Sidonians, Phoenicians, Philistines and Amorites.

It is time for the world to revisit the Old Testament with critical thinking minds and look at the contribution of the black nations — and Ham's descendants — from a proper perspective.

1.) What do you think about the broad spectrum of black nations contained in the Old Testament, according to Genesis 10? Why are the Hamite nations the most documented group of nations in the Old Testament?

2.) Why do you think the identities of Old Testament black nations were changed/altered to look like people of other races? Why is the modern world reluctant to reveal their true identities?

3.) After reading this chapter, how do you feel about white characters portrayed in Old Testament pictures instead of the true Hamite-black characters?

4.) How would humanity improve if people found out the truth about the Hamite nations in the Old Testament?

# 2

# Egypt, the Land of Ham

*"Princes shall come out of Egypt; Ethiopia shall soon stretch out her hands unto God."*

**Psalms 68:31**

**OBJECTIVE**

Egypt was one of the most documented nations listed in the Bible. This chapter will examine the Old Testament's clear position that Egypt was "The Land of Ham," belonging to the genealogy family of ancient black nations. The early beginnings of Egypt will shed light on its original connections to other black empires.

The Old Testament mentions Egypt more than 500 times. This impressive number of listings made Egypt one of the most talked-about countries. Genesis 10:6 lists the four sons of Ham:

*"And the sons of Ham; Cush, and Mizraim, and Phut, and Canaan."*

**Genesis 10:6**

Mizraim is the biblical ancestor-father of the Egyptian people. Mizraim is an old Hebrew word meaning "Egypt." Genesis 50:11 mentions Mizraim by name, showing the connection between him and Egypt.

*"And when the inhabitants of the land, the Canaanites, saw the mourning in the floor of Atad, they said, This is a grievous mourning to the Egyptians: wherefore the name of it was called 'Abelmizraim,' which is beyond Jordan."*

**Genesis 50:11**

The Old Testament mentioned Egypt as "the Land of Ham" in Psalms 78:51; Psalms 105:23; Psalms 105:26-27; and Psalms 106:21-22. The Old Testament writers were consistent in their association of Egypt with Ham's family of nations. There was no mention of Egypt belonging to the nations of Shem or Japheth:

*"And smote all the firstborn in Egypt; the chief of their strength in the tabernacles of Ham."*

**Psalms 78:51**

*"Israel also came into Egypt; and Jacob sojourned in the land of Ham."*

**Psalms 105:23**

*"He sent Moses his servant; and Aaron whom he had chosen. "They shewed his signs among them, and wonders in the land of Ham."*

**Psalms 105:26-27**

*"They forgot God their savior, which had done great things in Egypt; Wondrous works in the land of Ham, and terrible things by the Red Sea."*

**Psalms 106:21-22**

These verses consistently tied Egypt to the black nations — not to the Asiatic or white nations. The Old Testament continuously provides evidence of the presence of strong black nations. Modern scholars try to remove ancient Egypt as a land belonging to the black nations during the Old Testament era — which clearly contradicts the Old Testament writings. Prominent Egyptians in the Old Testament include:

- Moses' adopted mother and grandfather (Pharaoh).

- Hagar, the servant of Abraham and mother of his first-born son, Ishmael.
- Potiphar, the Egyptian captain of the Pharaoh's guard.
- Asenath, the Egyptian wife of Joseph.
- An unnamed daughter of Pharaoh, one of Solomon's primary wives.

## A Wide-Angle View of Egypt's Beginning

When upper and lower Egypt became unified around 3300 B.C., Egypt became a recognized empire and appeared onto the world stage at a rapid pace.

Within 800 years, Egypt had developed superior skills in astronomy, math, science, language, engineering and building practices. By 2500 B.C., Egypt had also erected its monumental pyramids, magnificent temples and grand statues.

During these ancient times, human progress and advancements moved at a slow, tedious pace. All advancements in science, math and engineering required development and human errors, then followed by continuous improvement over many centuries and perhaps millennia.

Modern history books do not show Egypt as receiving help or assistance from any previous empires as it rose to world prominence. Learning and copying from other nations was a common trait among newly formed empires.

However, historians credit Egypt with developing its civilization without help from other prominent nations that served as mentors-teachers. Egypt is probably the only biblical era empire credited with this unique civilization development autonomy of "we did it all by ourselves."

Egypt's autonomous-independent claim of rapid superior civilization development from 3300 to 2500 B.C. is simply too short of a timeline period. Eight centuries is not enough time to have developed their high-level culture that surpassed all other nations.

The Sphinx and the pyramids are evidence of a methodical and continuous civilization that was much older than Egypt. This ancient civilization developed for perhaps thousands of years and was not waiting for the country called Egypt to arrive and claim worldly attention. The Sphinx carries the face of a black man, one of ancient Ethiopian features.

**CHALLENGING QUESTION**

Did Egypt have "civilization teachers" from whom they borrowed for its quick rise in developing its civilization?

**CHALLENGING QUESTION**

Was Egypt ever part of an older empire from which it learned some of their early skills and disciplines?

## Ethiopian Empire's Impact on Egypt

At 3300 B.C., the Cushite (Ethiopian) empire was well established and much older than Egypt. Genesis 10 says Nimrod and his Cushite people were the early settlers in Mesopotamia (called "the Cradle of Civilization") and Assyria. The Ethiopians controlled the old Arabian lands and islands surrounding the Mediterranean Sea.

Ancient history and Old Testament scriptures connect Ethiopia and Egypt. The Ethiopians taught Egypt for many centuries before Egypt's establishment as a separate nation. The remnants of the connection between Ethiopia and Egypt continued for many more centuries as Egypt sprang forward into greatness.

According to Diodorus Siculus, a Greek historian from the first century B.C., the early culture, laws and religious practices of the ancient Egyptians closely resembled the Ethiopians.[12]

12. Houston, Drusilla Dunjee (1985). Wonderful Ethiopians of the Ancient Cushite Empire. Baltimore, MD: Black Classics Press. Page 68.

Sir Wallis Budge, the 19th-century Egyptologist, said that ancient Egyptian religious origins came from black nations and not from Asiatic nations.[13]

Drucilla Dunjee Houston, noted 20th-century historian, reported that ancient records pointed to Egypt as a colony of the Ethiopian empire.[14]

Historian and 19th-century Egyptologist William Flinders Petrie supported the belief that the ancient Egyptians did not have an Asiatic origin but were influenced by African-Hamite people.[15]

Houston later reported the Pharaohs of the early dynasties were black and resembled the Ethiopians.[16] They led Egypt's development in art, sculpturing, religion and architecture.

## Ethiopian and Egypt Biblically Connected

The Old Testament writers linked the Ethiopians and Egyptians in Bible verses. Both countries had ancient, historical ties to each other as they influenced the regions and lands around them. These two nations interfaced through shared religious customs, migrations of people between the lands, commercial trade and continuous military battles and wars.

These shared scripture verses revealed that these writers were aware of these two nations' connection:

> *"Princes shall come out of Egypt; Ethiopia shall soon stretch out her hands unto God."*
>
> **Psalms 68:31**

> *"For I am the Lord thy God, the Holy One of Israel, thy Saviour: I gave Egypt for thy ransom, Ethiopia and Seba for thee. Since thou wast precious in my sight, thou hast*

13. Houston, Drusilla Dunjee (1985). Wonderful Ethiopians of the Ancient Cushite Empire. Baltimore, MD: Black Classics Press. Page 83.
14. Ibid., Page 28.
15. Ibid., Pages 15, 68.
16. Ibid., Pages 93-94.

*been honourable, and I have loved thee: therefore, will I give men for thee, and people for thy life."*

**Isaiah 43:3-4**

*"Behold, therefore I am against thee, and against thy rivers, and I will make the land of Egypt utterly waste and desolate, from the tower of Syene even unto the border of Ethiopia."*

**Ezekiel 29:10**

*"Are ye not as children of the Ethiopians unto me, O children of Israel?" saith the Lord. "Have not I brought up Israel out of the land of Egypt? And the Philistines from Caphtor, and the Syrians from Kir?"*

**Amos 9:7**

Old Testament writers understood Egypt's connection to Ethiopia because both nations came from the same ancestral family tree of Ham, making them related.

## Black Pharaohs Led Egypt to Greatness

From approximately 3200 B.C. to 332 B.C., Egypt was led by rulers called pharaohs. Pharaohs were grouped into reigning periods or dynasties based on shared or common ancestry or a shared ruling philosophy. Each dynasty usually ruled until they were forcibly removed from the throne, such as uprisings or social and political upheaval. There were 30 main dynasties listed in Egyptian history.

From the beginnings of this unified nation, Egypt was led by powerful black pharaohs who seemingly were connected in ancestry with the ancient Ethiopian empire. Archived ancient statues and carvings of pharaohs from the early dynasties show facial features closely aligned with black people.

The early beginnings of Egypt consisted of a majority population of black people and this continued throughout the Old Testament era. Each time Egypt rose to high worldly prominence, black pharaohs were prominent among the rulers. When the black Pharaohs relinquished the throne to Asiatic influence, there was usually a slowdown or period of decline in Egypt's growth and world prominence.

SHUTTERSTOCK
**Statue of Pharaoh Khufu in the Cairo Egyptian Museum in Cairo, Egypt.**

Three dynasties stand out in the dynasties of pharaohs. The Fourth Dynasty (2610 B.C. to 2484 B.C.) ruled during a high achieving period called the golden age of the old Egyptian kingdom era. This period was the high point of pyramid building and a brilliant era of engineering feats in Egyptian history.

The pharaohs of this dynasty had Ethiopian physical features. The first ruler, Pharaoh Sneferu, built the Red Pyramid and Bent Pyramid. The second ruler of this dynasty, Pharaoh Khufu, built the Great Pyramid of Giza. Ancient statues show Khufu with distinct Ethiopian looking features. A third ruler, Pharaoh Khafre, built a pyramid named after him.

The Twelfth Dynasty ruled from 1990 B.C. to 1800 B.C. during the Middle Kingdom, a period of political division in Egypt. This group of notable black pharaohs included Amenemhat I, Amenemhat II and Senusret II. This dynasty revived the golden age of Egypt with a renewed interest in the arts and magnificent architecture. Before this dynasty, Egypt had declined and slowed economic growth.

Around 1700 B.C., a group of Asiatic people called the Hyksos invaded and conquered Egypt, ruling roughly 300 years. During this period, Egyptian civilization degraded rapidly into one of its darkest cultural periods. The Hyksos added little value to Egypt's vast history, destroying iconic temples and monuments. They were eventually driven out of the country by new Egyptian rulers.

The next great dynasty to rise in Egypt was led by black pharaohs in the Eighteenth Dynasty (1550-1290 B.C.). They restored Egypt's prominence in commerce, architecture and military.

SHUTTERSTOCK
**Statue of Pharaoh Thutmose III near the Festival Hall of Thutmose III at The Karnak Temple Complex in Luxor, Egypt.**

Thutmose III (1479-1425 B.C.) was the greatest of the pharaohs of this era, with many historians considering him the greatest pharaoh. He built numerous monuments and rebuilt the navy to a superior level to where Egypt became recognized again as the greatest country during biblical times. Thutmose III also erected many buildings in the southern territories of Nubia, more than any other pharaoh.

Thutmose III expanded the Egyptian empire internationally. He captured Nubia (which includes present-day Sudan) and the Asian regions of southern Syria and Canaan, along with areas on the Euphrates River. Thutmose III captured 350 cities during his reign. Other black pharaohs during the Eighteenth Dynasty include Amenhotep II and Amenhotep III.

## Summary

While there were Asiatic people who lived in the ancient Egyptian regions, the Old Testament writers consistently called Egypt "the

Land of Ham." The Old Testament writers stood as a testimony to the ancient black nation called Egypt.

Multiple nations conquered Egypt over time and its people became a blended ethnic mixture resulting from human migrations and invasions. But the dynamic engine that led to ancient Egypt's greatness was fueled by its black population.

## CHALLENGING QUESTION

Why do modern historians and scholars go to such great intellectual steps to remove ancient Egypt as a black nation?

## TALKING POINTS

The Old Testament mentioned Egypt as "the Land of Ham" in Psalms 78:51, Psalms 105: 23, Psalms 105: 26-27 and Psalms 106: 21-22. Moreover, the repopulation of the earth's genealogy, as stated in Genesis 10, assigned Egypt to the family tree of Ham.

1.) Why is the modern world obsessed with making ancient Egypt an Asian- or white-related nation when the Old Testament writers called ancient Egypt "the Land of Ham?"

2.) Why do you think the modern world is reluctant to accept that ancient Egypt was a black nation?

3.) Egypt is one of the most documented nations in the Old Testament, with more than 500 references. How do you feel your opinion of ancient Egypt would change if the world recognizes it as a black nation?

3

# Ethiopia, the Land of Wonders

*"Homer and Herodotus call all peoples of the Sudan, Egypt, Arabia, Palestine and Western Asia and India—Ethiopians."*

**Sir E.A. Wallis Budge**[17]

## OBJECTIVE

This chapter will explore the breadth and dominance of the Ethiopian empire and examine its influence on early world civilization. Old Testament-era events, characters and stories will substantiate Ethiopia's sustained position as a world leader.

One of the most powerful and misunderstood biblical empires was the Cush (Ethiopian) kingdom. While Egypt received a worldwide spotlight for historical achievements, Ethiopia was also advanced. This chapter will focus on the Ethiopian presence in the Old Testament, including a profile of Tirhakah, ruler over Egypt.

17. Jackson, John G. (1939). Ethiopia and the Origin of Civilization. Baltimore, MD: Black Classic Press. Page 8.

Chapters 4-6 will include profiles of Nimrod, the warrior and founder of Mesopotamia; Makeda, also known as the legendary Queen of Sheba; and Ebedmelech, the eunuch credited for saving the prophet Jeremiah from death.

The ancient name for this empire was Cush and the people were the Cushites. The Cushite empire dated to 5000 B.C. and included Sudan (also called Nubia), Libya, present-day Ethiopia, Mesopotamia region, parts of old Arabia and the Mediterranean islands.

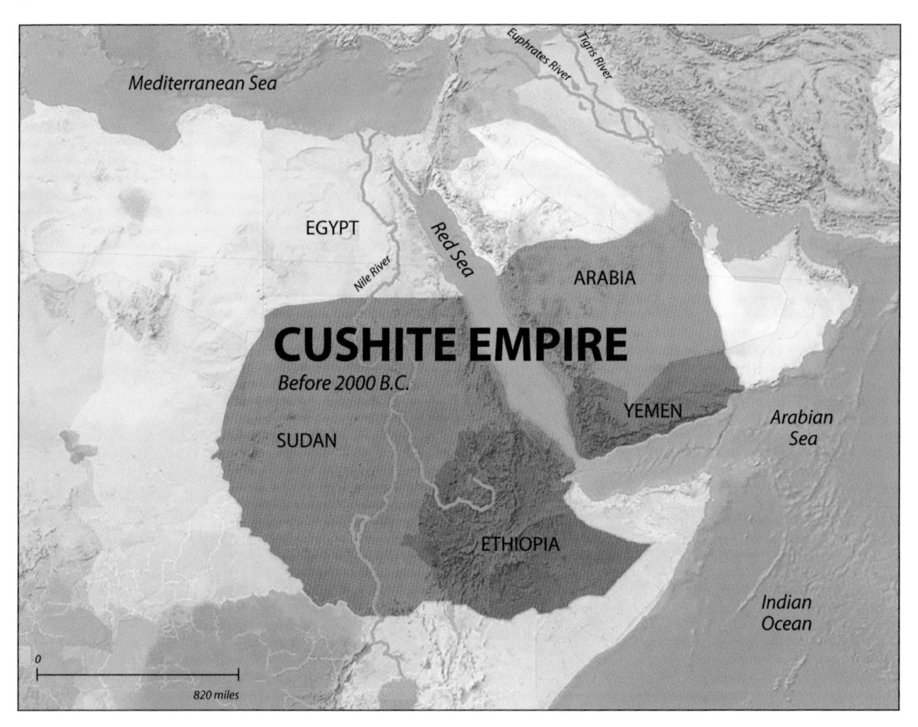


The Ethiopian empire is one of the oldest empires of the biblical era. The Ethiopians were ancestrally related to the Egyptians, Canaanites and ancient Babylonians as recorded in Genesis 10.

The Ethiopians were an expanding and conquering people who left their cultural imprint in many regions of the Old Testament world. Many of their stories centered around their constant travels and interactions with other nations, such as Israel, Babylon and Egypt. The Ethiopians were successful commercial merchants. They carried gold, incense, perfumes and precious stones such as topaz and emeralds to neighboring countries. Egypt and Israel were not naturally abundant in gold and incense, so they relied on the Ethiopians to supply them with these precious commodities.

A biblical example of Ethiopian travels and riches is in 1 Kings 10. In this story, the Ethiopian Queen Makeda (also called the Queen of Sheba), traveled with her caravan to visit King Solomon in Jerusalem. She presented him with a vast treasure of gold and other riches:

> *"And she gave the king a hundred and twenty talents of gold, and of spices very great store, and precious stones: there came no more such abundance of spices as these which the queen of Sheba gave to king Solomon."*
>
> **1 Kings 10:10**

The Old Testament mentioned the Ethiopians more than 50 times, often as royal leaders, military generals and commercial traders of precious commodities. The biblical writers were very aware of the high status placed on this legendary empire and they included this nation regularly in their stories.

Greek classical writers in the ninth century B.C. translated the empire's ancient name of Cush to the modern name of Ethiopia. The Greek term Ethiopia meant "a man with a sun-burned or black face."[18] The translation recognized the noticeable dark-skinned people living in the nation. For the context of this book, the terms "Ethiopia" and "Cush " are synonymous. The words "Ethiopia" and "Ethiopians" will mostly be used when referencing this nation.

References to the old Cushite empire are included in ancient Egyptian inscriptions under the word "Kash." In ancient Assyrian writings, the term for Cush was "Kushu." Variations of the word also include "Kush." [19]

18. Hansberry, William Leo (1981). Africa and Africans as Seen by Classical Writers, Vol. 2. Washington, D.C.: Howard University Press. Pages 6, 24.
19. The Holy Bible, Black Heritage Edition: King James Version (1976). Nashville, TN: Today, Inc. Page 72.

The prominence of the Ethiopian empire during early biblical days was present in Genesis. Ethiopia was the first significant nation listed in the Bible:

> *"And the name of the second river is Gihon: the same is it that compasseth the whole land of Ethiopia."*
>
> **Genesis 2:13**

Havilah, a land connected to the Ethiopians, was listed in Genesis 2:12, but Havilah by itself was not considered a significant nation.

**CHALLENGING QUESTION**

Why did the Old Testament writers mention Ethiopia, a black nation, so early in Genesis? Was this a coincidence or an important reference statement?

## The Ethiopian Presence

Nothing was coincidental or casual about the Ethiopian presence in the Bible. This initial statement in Genesis was a written testament to the strong legacy of Ethiopia. From the beginnings of Genesis and throughout the Old Testament, stories described the Ethiopians as world leaders in civilization and advancement.

Historians across the centuries were aware of the Ethiopian empire's historical presence. Examples of Ethiopian royalty in the Bible include Queen Candace in Acts 8:26-28 and King Tirhakah in II Kings 19:8-9 and Isaiah 37:9-10. Their written stories and testimonies agree with the Old Testament accounts of Ethiopia. Stephanus of Byzantium from the sixth century A.D. voiced his universal declaration about Ethiopia:

> *"Ethiopia was the first established country on Earth and the Ethiopians were the first to set up the worship of the gods and to establish laws."*[20]

20. Houston, Drusilla Dunjee (1985). Wonderful Ethiopians of the Ancient Cushite Empire. Baltimore, MD: Black Classics Press. Page 17.

A.H. Heeren (1760-1842), a European historian who provided research and valuable information on ancient Ethiopia, stated:

> *"From the remotest times to the present, the Ethiopians have been the most celebrated and yet the most mysterious of nations. In the earliest traditions of the more civilized nations of antiquity, the name of this most distant people is found. The annals of the Egyptian priests were full of them, and the nations of inner Asia on the Euphrates and the Tigris have woven the fictions of the Ethiopians with their own traditions of the wars and conquests of their heroes."*[21]

Christian Charles Josias von Bunsen (1791-1860), a 19th-century German scholar, said:

> *"The Hamitic family as Rawlinson proves must be given the credit for being the fountainhead of civilization. This family comprised the ancient Ethiopians, the Egyptians, the original Canaanites and the old Chaldeans. The inscriptions of the Chaldean monuments prove their race affinity."*[22]

Bunsen also said the following about Cushite expansion:

> *"Cushite colonies were all along the southern shores of Asia and Africa and by the archaeological remains, along the southern and eastern coasts of Arabia. The name Cush was given to four great areas, Media, Persia, Susiana and Aria, or the whole territory between the Indus and Tigris in prehistoric times. In Africa, the Ethiopians, the Egyptians, the Libyans, the Canaanites and Phoenicians were all descendants of Ham. They were a black or dark colored race and the pioneers of our civilization. They were emphatically the monument builders on the plains of Shinar and the valley of the Nile from Meroe to Memphis."*[23]

British author and historian Thomas Maurice (1754-1824) stated in his book "History of Hindostan:"

---

21. Houston, Drusilla Dunjee (1985). Wonderful Ethiopians of the Ancient Cushite Empire. Baltimore, MD: Black Classics Press. Page 24.
22. Ibid., Page 19.
23. Ibid., Page 20.

*"When the daring Cushite genius was in the full career of its glory, it was the peculiar delight of this enterprising race to erect stupendous edifices, excavate long subterranean passages in the living rock, form vast lakes and extend over the hollows of adjoining mountains magnificent arches for aqueducts and bridges. It was they who built the tower of Babel or Belus and raised the pyramids (of) Egypt; ... Their skill in mechanical powers astonishes posterity, who are unable to conceive by what means stones thirty, forty and even sixty feet in length from twelve to twenty in depth could ever be raised to the point of elevation at which they are seen in the ruined temples of Belbec and Thebais."*[24]

## Ethiopia and Egypt Biblically Connected

As shown in Chapter Two, the Old Testament writers linked the Ethiopians and Egyptians in Bible verses. Both countries had ancient, historical ties to each other as they influenced the regions and lands around them. The Book of Psalms provides a compelling example of how God was in touch with these two Hamite-black nations:

*"Princes shall come out of Egypt; Ethiopia shall soon stretch out her hands unto God."*

**Psalms 68:31**

In the first part of the verse, the biblical writers connected Egypt and Ethiopia. The second part of the verse signifies that Ethiopia had a special relationship with God. The stretching out of hands in biblical days was often a spiritual and positive sign of acknowledgment and reverence.

Also note the use of "her hands" within this verse. The traditional masculine gender was the preferred writing method in biblical days. Referencing a powerful nation with a female gender was a unique and special biblical notation.[25]

This last verse recorded a connection between India and Ethiopia, showing Ethiopia's large presence in the Old Testament:

24. Houston, Drusilla Dunjee (1985). Wonderful Ethiopians of the Ancient Cushite Empire. Baltimore, MD: Black Classics Press. Page 38.
25. The Holy Bible, Black Heritage Edition: King James Version (1976). Nashville, Tenn.: Today, Inc. P. 85.

> *"Now it came to pass in the days of Ahasuerus, (this is Ahasuerus which reigned, from India even unto Ethiopia, over a hundred and seven and twenty provinces)."*
>
> **Esther 1:1**

## Ethiopia's Military Might

The Ethiopians were known for their strong armies and strategic prowess during wars and battles. Ancient history records refer to them as fierce warriors, with soldiers unwilling to retreat during the toughest of battles. Their military records carried a long list of conquests and victories.

The Second Book of Chronicles 14:8-13 recorded a historic battle between the Israelites and Ethiopians. The Israelites under their leader Asa carried a large army into action equipped with shields, bows and spears. This army involved the tribes of Judah and Benjamin.

Their opponents were the Ethiopians, led by their mighty general Zerah. The Bible stated that the Ethiopian army consisted of "a thousand, thousand soldiers," a number that represents 1 million soldiers in the Ethiopian army. While it is unsure whether the Bible meant 1 million Ethiopian soldiers showed up for this battle or there were 1 million men in the Ethiopian army, this was the largest military of any nation recorded in the Old Testament:

> *"And Asa had an army of men that bare targets and spears, out of Judah three hundred thousand; and out of Benjamin, that bare shields and drew bows, two hundred and fourscore thousand: all these were mighty men of valour.*
>
> *"And there came out against them Zerah the Ethiopian with a host of a thousand thousand, and three hundred chariots, and came unto Mareshah."*
>
> **2 Chronicles 14:8-9**

Some takeaways from the battle that provide insight to the Ethiopian army's might, as detailed in 2 Chronicles 14:8-13:

- The Ethiopians had a more advanced and prepared army.
- The Ethiopian army had 300 chariots, while the Israelites did not have chariots (2 Chronicles 14:9). The first reference of the Israelites using chariots appeared in later centuries during the rule of David in the 10th century B.C.
- The Ethiopians had traveled hundreds of miles into the Israelites lands in the valley of Zephathah at Mareshah. (2 Chronicles 14:9-10).
- Asa, from the Israelites, cried out to God for divine help (2 Chronicles 14:11).
- Asa said the Israelites could not defeat the Ethiopians with just their strength (2 Chronicles 14:11).
- God intervened to help the Israelites defeat the Ethiopians (2 Chronicles 14:12).
- The Bible said that God, not the Israelites, defeated the Ethiopians (2 Chronicles 14:12-13).

**CHALLENGING QUESTION**

Why did "the chosen people" of Israel need God's help to defeat the Ethiopians? Why did the Israelites confess in 2 Chronicles 14: 11 that "They were powerless against the Ethiopians?"

The Ethiopian empire would need a reliable infrastructure of social systems, sound agriculture management, solid economic stability, sound government and stable family order practices to support an army of 1 million soldiers. To maintain an army of this size provides evidence of the historical stature of this nation.

However, the Ethiopians' greatest military rivals were not the Israelites but the Egyptians, with whom they waged many wars throughout millennia. The Ethiopians won many of these wars, but they also lost some costly encounters with their Egyptian neighbors. The Ethiopians spent considerable time, energy and resources consumed with warfare. They were in constant wars and over time, these excessive military practices did contribute to the decline of their kingdom.

## Ethiopia Helps Save the Israelites

There were times in the Old Testament when Ethiopia was an ally of Israel. During the reign of Israelite King Hezekiah in seventh century B.C., the Assyrian empire planned war and destruction on Jerusalem. The Assyrian king received reports that the Ethiopian king Tirhakah, ruler over Egypt and Ethiopia, planned to join forces with the Israelites. By this time, the Ethiopians had conquered Egypt and Tirhakah's army included both Egyptian and Ethiopian soldiers.

The Ethiopians and Israelites had a common enemy in Assyria. This alliance could account for their combined forces that fought against the Assyrians in the biblical narratives.

The Assyrians had also attempted to invade Egypt but failed in their initial battles against the Ethiopian and Egyptian armies. The following verses (2 Kings 19: 9-10, Isaiah 37: 9-10) chronicles Tirhakah and his desire to join forces with Hezekiah against the Assyrians:

> *"And when he heard say of Tirhakah king of Ethiopia, Behold, he is come out to fight against thee: he sent messengers again unto Hezekiah, saying ...*
>
> *"Thus shall ye speak to Hezekiah king of Judah, saying, Let not thy God in whom thou trust deceive thee, saying, Jerusalem shall not be delivered into the hand of the king of Assyria."*
>
> **2 Kings 19: 9-10**
>
> *"And he heard say concerning Tirhakah king of Ethiopia. He is come forth to make war with thee. And when he heard it, he sent messengers to Hezekiah, saying,*

*"Thus shall ye speak to Hezekiah king of Judah, saying, Let not thy God, in whom thou trust, deceive thee, saying, Jerusalem shall not be given into the hand of the king of Assyria."*

**Isaiah 37: 9-10**

## Profile on Tirhakah

Tirhakah (the biblical spelling for King Taharqa) was part of the Ethiopian dynasty that ruled over Egypt until the Assyrians defeated them. Taharqa ruled over both Ethiopia and Egypt during his reign (688 B.C.-662 B.C.).[26] Taharqa succeeded the legendary Ethiopian ruler Piankhi, who conquered Egypt during his reign of 753 B.C. to 713 B.C.

SHUTTERSTOCK

**Statue of Pharaoh Taharqa's face on a lion-figured sphinx in the British Museum in London.**

Taharqa was noted for his construction and cultural projects. He was credited with building several temples in present-day Sudan with one notable temple erected for the gods Osiris and Ptah. Taharqa maintained strong economic, religious and cultural connections between Egypt and Ethiopia.

The Assyrians ultimately were able to conquer Egypt and defeated Taharqa's armies, causing him to escape back into his southern Ethiopian lands.

---

26. Green, Richard L. (1988). A Salute to Historic African Kings and Queens. Chicago, IL: Empak Enterprises, Inc. Page 13.

## Other Ethiopian References

Additionally, Ethiopia's presence is prominent in other books in the Old Testament. Numbers 12:1 said that Moses married an Ethiopian woman:

> *"And Miriam and Aaron spake against Moses because of the Ethiopian woman whom he had married: for he had married an Ethiopian woman."*
>
> **Numbers 12:1**

Isaiah 18:1 acknowledged the presence of the Ethiopian empire:

> *"Woe to the land shadowing with wings, which is beyond the rivers of Ethiopia."*
>
> **Isaiah 18:1**

And there is Jeremiah 13: 23, which uses this metaphor:

> *"Can the Ethiopian change his skin, or the leopard his spots? Then may ye also do good, that are accustomed to do evil."*
>
> **Jeremiah 13:23**

## Architecture Splendors

The ancient Ethiopians erected monuments and temples in their lands, using engineering and building techniques that rivaled the monuments in Egypt. They built temples, palaces and pyramids and were known for detailed design work, intricate carvings and excellent quality craftsmanship. Examples of their ancient architecture works include:

**Jebel Barkal:** The name for the small mountain and archaeological site along the Nile River about 250 miles north of Khartoum, Sudan. Jebel Barkal is a primary archaeological site of the Cush kingdom that started around 1400 B.C. The location has more than 20 buildings, including at least 13 temples, some chapels and at least two palaces. Located nearby is a group of well-preserved royal pyramids.

**Nubian Pyramids:** Located within Sudan are approximately 225 pyramids constructed at three sites around 700 B.C. to 300 B.C. They served as tombs for kings and queens. The largest number of these pyramids are in the area of Meroë, where 40 queens and kings were

SHUTTERSTOCK
**Jebel Barkal is a mountain and archaeological site along the Nile River about 250 miles north of Khartoum, Sudan. Jebel Barkal is a primary archaeological site of the Cush kingdom.**

SHUTTERSTOCK
**Jebel Barkal has more than 20 buildings, including at least 13 temples, some chapels and at least two palaces. Pictured are some carvings from one of the locations.**

SHUTTERSTOCK
**Meroë, Sudan has the largest number of Nubian Pyramids, where 40 queens and kings were buried.**

buried. These pyramids are not as old as the Egyptian pyramids and range in heights from 20 to 100 feet (6 to 30 meters). This vast array of pyramids is another testimony to the ancient wonders of the Ethiopians.

## Summary

Ethiopia's constant presence in the Old Testament showed Old Testament writers had an eye on the Ethiopian empire. Although not part of the "chosen people," God had an affinity for this black nation. Ethiopia was a well-known, established and world leader during the Old Testament era. Old Testament writers knew of the splendors of the empire and frequently wrote about the Ethiopian people and their achievements.

## TALKING POINTS

Ethiopia is the oldest empire in the Old Testament — the first recognized prominent nation in the Bible (Genesis 2:13) — and was a leader in the early development of ancient world civilization. History shows Egypt was originally a colony of the Ethiopian empire, and the Ethiopians were Egypt's original teachers of civilization.

1.) How do you feel about the display of enormous wealth the Ethiopians possessed, as evidenced by the Queen of Sheba's visit to Jerusalem when she gave King Solomon a fortune of gold, precious stones and large amounts of spices (I Kings 10:2,10)?

2.) What do you think about the reference to another rich and powerful Ethiopian queen, Queen Candace, in Acts 8:27?

3.) Why were the Ethiopians featured in such prominent roles as queens, kings, great military leaders and vibrant commercial traders? Why would the Old Testament state the Ethiopian army had the largest military listed ("a thousand thousand"), as stated in II Chronicles 14:9?

# Hamite Leaders

Chapter 4: Nimrod,
Founder of Mesopotamia

Chapter 5: Makeda,
Queen of Sheba

Chapter 6: Ebedmelech,
the Ethiopian Servant

Chapter 7: The Land of Canaan

# Nimrod, Founder of Mesopotamia

*"What became of the Black People of Sumer?" the traveler asked the old man. "For ancient records show that the people of Sumer were Black. What happened to them?"*

*"Ah," the old man sighed. "They lost their history, so they died."*

**A Sumer Legend**[27]

## OBJECTIVE

This chapter will examine the iconic ancient civilization figure Nimrod, whose story is embedded directly into Noah's Great Flood story and repopulation of the earth. This chapter will expand on the stories and myths surrounding this popular world figure known throughout ancient Mesopotamia and Asiatic regions.

Nimrod didn't believe in God and he didn't do any recorded Bible deeds such as helping and feeding people. However, his presence as a historical figure was too significant to ignore and Old Testament authors included him in biblical writings.

27. Williams, Chancellor (1976). The Destruction of Black Civilization: Great Issues of a Race from 4500 B.C. to 2000 A.D. 13th ed. Chicago, IL: Third World Press. Page 15.

Nimrod was the son of Cush, the grandson of Ham and the great-grandson of Noah as recorded in Genesis 10 (Noah > Ham > Cush > Nimrod). Nimrod was a Cushite, the ancient name for the Ethiopians. Nimrod was a dominant ruler in ancient Mesopotamia and was legendary in Mesopotamian folklore, oral and traditional history. Nimrod also was called Belus in ancient Mesopotamia history.

From a traditional biblical perspective, Nimrod seems like an unlikely addition to the Bible. The Bible writings on Nimrod were not spiritual or religious narratives, but historical accounts in Genesis 10:8-12.

The first citing of Nimrod and his ancestry — identifying him as a member of the Cushite nation and belonging to the family tree of Noah's son Ham — are in Genesis 10:6 and 10:8:

> *"And the sons of Ham; Cush, and Mizraim, and Phut, and Canaan."*
>
> **Genesis 10:6**

> *"And Cush begat Nimrod: he began to be a mighty one in the earth."*
>
> **Genesis 10:8**

On the surface, Nimrod's narrative seems like a special insert into the Old Testament. His story was strictly about conquering and the expansion of people and their lands.

## CHALLENGING QUESTION

Why did the writers of Genesis 10 include Nimrod's story within these essential 30 genealogy verses about the repopulation of the earth? Why did Nimrod receive so many verses?

According to scriptures, Noah's sons and their descendants would repopulate the earth and that is what Nimrod did. Nimrod and his people led the repopulation of critical regions of the ancient Asiatic world, per the biblical plan:

> *"And God blessed Noah and his sons, and said unto them: Be fruitful, and multiply, and replenish the earth."*
>
> **Genesis 9:1**

In the Genesis10's telling about the earth's repopulation after the Great Flood, Nimrod received five verses for his achievements. It is remarkable since Noah's son Japheth, the ancestral father of all white nations, received only four verses.

## Profile: Nimrod

Nimrod was a high-achieving king who traveled across great distances and lands of the Old Testament. He and his Cushite people (the Ethiopians) did not live in Africa but instead resided in Asia (see map). Biblical black nations were conquering and expanding people.

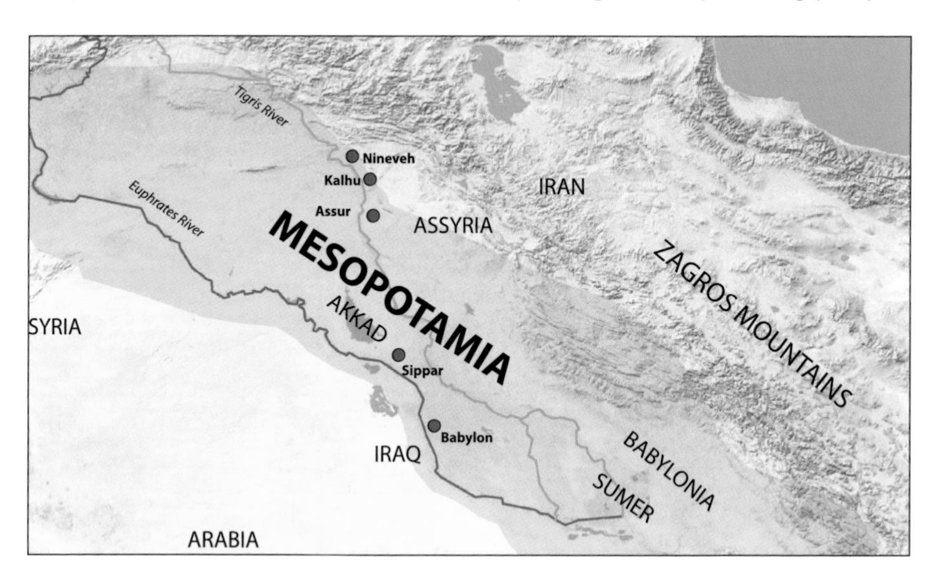


The Bible documented Nimrod's achievements and listed the cities that he founded. According to Genesis 10: 9-10, the original builders of early cities in Mesopotamia were Nimrod and the Cushites. Nimrod's kingdom was located within the lands of Shinar (Genesis 10:10), an old Hebrew term for the area called Mesopotamia. [28]

28. Brand, Chad; Draper, Charles; England, Archie (2003). Holman Illustrated Bible Dictionary. Nashville, TN: Holman Bible Publishers. Page 1489.

*"He was a mighty hunter before the Lord: wherefore it is said, Even as Nimrod the mighty hunter before the Lord.*

*"And the beginning of his kingdom was Babel, and Erech, and Accad, and Calneh, in the land of Shinar."*

**Genesis 10:9-10**

Babel (also known as Babylon) was part of old Mesopotamia and located in present-day Iraq. The cities that Nimrod founded are:

- **Babel:** Hebrew word meaning "confusion." Robert L. Cate, Phoebe Young professor of religious studies at Oklahoma State University, said it was the name of the city that Noah's disobedient descendants built, so they would not be scattered over all the earth. Babel became the Old Testament's symbol of rebellion. Babel was the older name for the area called Babylon.[29]
- **Erech:** Hebrew translation of Akkadian place-name. Uruk was an old Sumerian city founded before 3100 B.C. The Table of Nations reports that Nimrod included Erech in his kingdom.[30]
- **Accad:** The Mesopotamian city that founded the Akkadian language used by Babylon and Assyria.[31]
- **Calneh:** A part of Nimrod's kingdom.[32]

Babylon was mentioned more than 200 times in the Old Testament. This ancient city was much older than the Hebrew people and biblical writers. Babylon goes back to at least 3000 B.C. During the Old Testament era, there were latter Semitic tribes and conquering invasions that altered the original settlers living in the area. However, the initial beginnings of this eternal city belong to the descendants of Ham.

---

29. Brand, Chad; Draper, Charles; England, Archie (2003). Holman Illustrated Bible Dictionary. Nashville, TN: Holman Bible Publishers. Page 155.
30. Ibid., Page 502.
31. Ibid., Page 16.
32. Ibid., Page 254.

### CHALLENGING QUESTION

Why is the modern world so reluctant to acknowledge that the original inhabitants and builders of Mesopotamia (called "the Cradle of Civilization"), were the black nations of people?

In Nimrod's conquest and expansion, the Bible narrates in Genesis 10:11-12 that Nimrod continued and moved into ancient Assyria:

> *"Out of that land went forth Asshur, and builded Nineveh, and the city Rehoboth, and Calah.*
>
> *"And Resen between Nineveh and Calah: the same is a great city."*
>
> **Genesis 10:11-12**

The cities Nimrod founded during this period are:

- **Nineveh:** Edwin Yamauchi, professor of history at Miami (Ohio) University, called it a great city in the ancient Assyrian empire located on the Tigris River in northeastern Mesopotamia (modern-day Iraq).[33] It became the home of Sennacherib, king of Assyria.
- **Rehoboth:** Likely denotes a city located between Nineveh and Calah.[34]
- **Calah:** The city that Nimrod built.[35]
- **Resen:** Name meaning "fountainhead." The city that Nimrod founded between Nineveh and Calah. [36]

It is interesting to note that Genesis 10: 8-12 used the word "mighty"

33. Brand, Chad; Draper, Charles; England, Archie (2003). Holman Illustrated Bible Dictionary. Nashville, TN: Holman Bible Publishers. Page 1192.
34. Ibid., Page 1373.
35. Ibid., Page 250.
36. Ibid., Page 1379.

three times to describe Nimrod. First Chronicles 1:8-10 also provides a biblical recording of Nimrod.

## Nimrod's historical role

Nimrod's story occurred long before the development of the Assyrians and other Asiatic people in the Mesopotamian region. Being Cushite, Nimrod had access to the traditional culture of the old Cushite empire. He was knowledgeable in the agricultural, engineering, building and military strengths that the Cushites possessed.

Nimrod's legacy endured centuries after his death. The Book of Micah, written during the eighth century B.C., called Assyria "the land of Nimrod." It is notable considering Nimrod lived more than 2,000 years before the writing of Micah. Yet Nimrod's legacy was so widespread in Asiatic lands that biblical writers still associated his name with Assyria. Genesis 10:11-12 and Micah 5:6 both credit Nimrod as the early settler in the region of Assyria.

> *"And they shall waste the land of Assyria with the sword, and the land of Nimrod in the entrances thereof: thus shall he deliver us from the Assyrian, when he cometh into our land, and when he treadeth within our borders."*
>
> **Micah 5:6**

**DID YOU KNOW?**

The city Nimrud was an ancient Assyrian city located south of the city of Mosul, named after Nimrod. It was a major Assyrian city between 1350 B.C. and 610 B.C., and still exists today.

## Tower of Babel

Nimrod and his people were also believed to be the creators of the biblical Tower of Babel. Ancient Babylon folklore associated the building of the Tower of Babel to Nimrod as a testament to his rebellious and authoritarian lifestyle. First-century Jewish-Roman historian Flavius Josephus wrote that Nimrod probably built the Tower of Babel.[37]

Not only was Nimrod listed in the Bible, but the ancient history of the Mesopotamian region recognized his legendary status. There are oral stories, inscriptions about him and written history that support the legacy of Nimrod. The ancient history tales of Chaldea and Mesopotamia called him a mighty ruler and conqueror.

Over the centuries, historians and scholars confirmed the impact of Nimrod's legacy in Mesopotamia. Their research and conclusions agree with Genesis 10:

- **Drusilla Dunjee Houston**, 20th-century historian, author and researcher, stated that "Belus (Nimrod), king of Chaldea serves to unite the Chaldeans with the Old Race of the Upper Nile, as does their building the temple of Anu, another name of the original Cushite family."[38]
- **Moses of Chorene** (410-490s A.D.), the Armenian historian, identified Belus, a great king of Babylon, as possibly being Nimrod. Moses cited the connection between Babylonia and Ethiopia, stating the Babylonian region and its formations were in honor of Belus and Cush.[39]
- **George Rawlinson**, the 19th-century English scholar and historian, said:

---

37. Josephus, Flavius; Whiston, William (translator); Boer, Paul A. (editor) (2014). The Antiquities of the Jews: Volume I (Books I - X) (Vol. 1). Scotts Valley, CA: CreateSpace Independent Publishing Platform. Page 81.
38. Houston, Drusilla Dunjee (1985). Wonderful Ethiopians of the Ancient Cushite Empire. Baltimore, MD: Black Classics Press. Page 161.
39. Ibid., Page 163.

*"The strength of Nimrod's character and the greatness of his achievements are remarkably indicated by a variety of testimonies, which place him among the foremost characters of the ancient world. At least as early as the time of Moses, his name had passed into proverb. He was known as the mighty hunter before the lord. In his own nation, he was deified and continued down to the latest times as the chief object of worship. In Arabian tradition, Nimrod played a conspicuous part. Orion in the Arabian astronomy bears his title. His name lives in the tales of the people of Chaldea today. Wherever a mound is to be seen in Babylon or the adjoining countries, the local tradition attaches to it the name of Nimrod. The most striking ruins of the upper and lower Mesopotamian valley are thus made the monuments of his glory (p. 82)."* [40]

**CHALLENGING QUESTION**

Why is modern humanity not able to realize that the black nations were at the beginnings and the fountainhead of early civilization?

## Impacts of Nimrod and Cushites on Mesopotamia

The Mesopotamia plains were approximately 300 miles long and 150 miles wide. The Tigris and Euphrates rivers flowed through the area. Early settlements date back to about 5000 B.C., with more cities emerging around 4000 B.C. and cultural development maintained around 3000 B.C.

The early beginnings of Mesopotamian civilization cannot be credited to the early Asiatic tribes living in the region. There is no evidence of Semites developing continuous high-level cities or sustained architectural and engineering knowledge during the third and fourth millennia B.C.

40. Houston, Drusilla Dunjee (1985). Wonderful Ethiopians of the Ancient Cushite Empire. Baltimore, MD: Black Classics Press. Page 165.

Berosus, a noted historian and priest, who lived in the Babylon region during the third century B.C., wrote *Babyloniaca (History of Babylonia).* In addition, Berosus concluded that the Cushite people brought civilization into ancient Mesopotamia instead of the nomadic Semite tribes that also inhabited the region.

The Old Testament records in Genesis 10 substantiate that the Cushites settled in Mesopotamia during the earliest times. Everywhere the Cushites went, they established cities, built large monuments and managed large rivers. This pattern was part of the larger Cushite civilization that extended throughout the ancient world.

The primary area of Mesopotamia was divided into two separate regions. The northern region called Accad included early Babel (Babylon), while the southern division was called Sumer, which included Erech, Ur and Chaldea. The first inhabitants of both areas— the northern Accadians and the southern Sumerians — were part of the Cushite nations.

## Babylon

In the northern area, Babylon enjoyed a vibrant culture, maintained magnificent temples and built palaces on platforms high above the ground. The buildings were made of high-quality bricks. The tallest building in ancient Babylon was the great temple of Belus, with an estimated height of 500 feet.

At the top of the temple was a giant statue of Bel (another name for Nimrod). These remarkable engineering feats relied on Cushite methods and techniques learned from their ancestral people.

Large palaces existed, covered in gold decor and intricately carved ornaments. Babylon was called "The Golden City" in the biblical Old Testament:

> *"That thou shalt take up this proverb against the king of Babylon, and say, How hath the oppressor ceased! The golden city ceased!"*
>
> **Isaiah 14:4**

## Chaldea

Ancient tales of Chaldea named Nimrod as the founder of the region. Chaldea was located in the southeastern part of Mesopotamia and geographically is part of modern-day Iraq. The early inhabitants were the Sumerians, who developed city-states around 5000 B.C. The Sumerians developed the first form of writing called cuneiform, which was later adopted by Semite tribes.

The ancient Chaldeans were knowledgeable about stars, comets and early astronomy. Starting around 2200 B.C., they maintained continuous astronomy records for more than 1500 consecutive years. The origins of modern western world astronomy are believed to come from Mesopotamia.

The emergence of strong Asiatic nations became visible around 2300 B.C. as they began to control large regions of Mesopotamian lands. Their accomplishments to civilization were significant, but the black nations of people created the original civilization infrastructure for Mesopotamian success.

## Summary

Nimrod was legendary throughout ancient Mesopotamia history. His building feats were outstanding with the remarkable list of cities that he founded, as some of his cities became great symbols in the Old Testament era.

In ancient Mesopotamia, there were cities and statues named in Nimrod's honor. Even though his biblical story did not demonstrate any spirituality connections to anyone, still his iconic, historical presence was too significant for even the Old Testament writers to overlook.

## TALKING POINTS

Nimrod was the iconic Cushite founder of the ancient Mesopotamian region; he was too prominent of a figure not to be recognized by Old Testament writers. Nimrod's story appears in Genesis 10, the essential story about the repopulation of the earth after the Great Flood.

1.) Nimrod was not considered a spiritual leader nor a traditional Old Testament character. Why do you think Nimrod's story received such high status in the Genesis 10 genealogy?

2.) Micah 5:6 called Assyria "the land of Nimrod," in addition to Nimrod being credited as the founder of Babylon and Nineveh (Genesis 10:10-11). How would you describe Nimrod's unique presence in the Old Testament?

# 5

# Makeda, Queen of Sheba

*"I **am** black, but comely, O ye daughters of Jerusalem, as the tents of Kedar, as the curtains of Solomon.*

*"Look not upon me, because I **am** black, because the sun hath looked upon me."*

**Songs of Solomon 1:5, 6**

## OBJECTIVE

This chapter covers the legendary Ethiopian Queen Makeda (also called the Queen of Sheba), whose biblical queen status is only surpassed by Queen Esther in the Old Testament. This section will showcase her life and her famous travels to Jerusalem using ancient Ethiopian manuscripts and biblical references. Finally, the chapter will highlight the Ethiopians' unique perspective of having female rulers.

A unique aspect of the Ethiopian empire was its leadership under female rulers who demonstrated courage, wisdom and diplomacy equaled to kingdoms that were led by traditional kings. The biblical era records the presence of Ethiopian queens from 1000 B.C. through at least the third century A.D.

The Bible recorded the Ethiopian queens known for their high-level commercial trade. An example was the Candace queen listed in the New Testament in Acts 8:26-28. In a brief story, the apostle Phillip encountered a high-level Ethiopian business official who was traveling through Jerusalem.

The queen in the story possibly was named Amantitere. There was a strong line of eight Ethiopian queens that carried the title of Candace.

> *26 "And the angel of the Lord spake unto Philip, saying, Arise, and go toward the south unto the way that goeth down from Jerusalem unto Gaza, which is desert.*
>
> *27 "And he arose and went: and, behold, a man of Ethiopia, an eunuch of great authority under Candace queen of the Ethiopians, who had the charge of all her treasure, and had come to Jerusalem for to worship,*
>
> *28 "Was returning, and sitting in his chariot read Esaias the prophet."*
>
> **Acts 8:26-28**

In these verses, we learn about:

- Queen Candace and the wealth of her empire.
- Her commerce leader— an Ethiopian man — who was riding in a chariot, an evident sign of prominence.
- Her commerce leader was very literate and reading biblical material.
- Her commerce leader was in Jerusalem, which was a long way from his Ethiopian homelands.

## Profile: The Candace Queens

The Candace Queens were a grouping of female rulers of the ancient Cushite (Ethiopian) empire who ruled before and after the birth of Christ. Some of these queens were in the area called Meroe, which is part of present-day Sudan. The title "Candace" is historically found along with the similar title versions "Kentake" or "Kandake."

The Candace Queens were:

- Shanakdakhete (r.c. 170 BCE)
- Amanirenas (r.c. 40-10 BCE)
- Amanishakheto (r.c. 10 BCE-1 C.E.)
- Amanitore (r.c. 1-c. 25 C.E.)
- Amantitere (r.c. 25-c. 41 C.E.)
- Amanikhatashan (r.c. 62-c. 85 C.E.)
- Maleqorobar (r.c. 266-c. 283 CE)
- Lahideamani (r.c. 306-c. 314 CE)

**NOTE:** BCE stands for "Before the Common Era" and is an alternative to B.C. (before the birth of Christ). C.E. stands for "Common Era," which is an alternative to A.D. (after the death of Christ).

Even though most of the Candace Queens were not in the Bible, their unique positions of female leadership during ancient Biblical days is too significant to ignore and deserves recognition.

## Makeda, Queen of Sheba

The most prominent of the Ethiopian queens lived about 1,000 years before the Candace queens: Makeda, the legendary Queen of Sheba. She was a powerful leader of the Ethiopian empire whose influence spread throughout Israel, Egypt and neighboring countries.

Makeda has several citings in the Bible: 1 Kings 10:1-13 and 2 Chronicles 9:1-12 in the Old Testament; and Matthew 12:42 in the New Testament. Additionally, she appears in the Qur'an, where she is called "Queen of the South." Makeda is the only historical queen to be listed in the Old Testament, the New Testament and the Qur'an.

## Makeda's Story

Makeda was born into the Ethiopian royal family around the time 1000 B.C. to King Kawnasya and Queen Ismenie. When her older brother Rouz died tragically in a fire as a young boy, Makeda became the sole heir to the throne. After King Kawnasya's death, Makeda became queen at age 16.

During Queen Makeda's nearly 50-year reign:

- She developed strong commercial trade with regional countries such as Israel and Egypt.
- She promoted international diplomacy and ongoing peace with neighboring lands.
- She provided strong economic stability for her empire.
- She also shared the country's wealth with her people from all socioeconomic backgrounds.

During the reign of King Solomon, the Ethiopian empire established strong ties with Israel, especially in the areas of commercial trading. The Ethiopians had an abundance of gold, perfumes, incense and regularly sold those items to King Solomon and the Israelite people.

Makeda received her secondary title of "Queen of Sheba" from the legendary abundance of minerals, mines and precious stones found in the regions of the kingdom called Seba.

While the Bible told a brief story of the queen, the most significant recording of Makeda's history is in the ancient Ethiopian manuscript, the Kebra Nagast. This manuscript — which is more than 1,000 years old and found in a cave — is highly treasured in Ethiopian culture and contains biographical accounts of several prominent Ethiopian leaders, including Queen Makeda. The Kebra Nagast's accounts and the Bible share common information.

The Kebra Nagast talked about how the Ethiopians possessed 300 ships and many camel caravans, which carried out their significant export business demands for precious commodities. During their extensive business dealings, Ethiopian commerce leaders learned about the extraordinary wisdom and knowledge of King Solomon. Such observations and stories made their way back to the Ethiopian leaders, which led to Makeda's desire to visit Jerusalem.

The Kebra Nagast described the planning needed to make such a long, arduous journey to Jerusalem. Makeda's kingdom was approximately 1,500 miles away from Jerusalem. The travel time took as long as nine months each way, mostly through the desert. An army of soldiers, servants and helpers joined the large caravan making the journey.

**CHALLENGING QUESTION**

Why has the world been so reluctant to acknowledge that the Queen of Sheba was a black queen from a black nation? Why hide this information from worldwide readers who are searching for expanded biblical knowledge?

## Makeda's Journey to Jerusalem

Makeda's journey to Jerusalem to visit King Solomon and the events of this historic meeting is in 1 Kings 10: 1-13. The first verses detail the enormous riches and treasures that Makeda gave to Solomon. The queen challenged the king with intellectual debate and hard questions (1 Kings 10: 1-3).

Makeda later stayed in Jerusalem as a guest. According to the Kebra Nagast, she studied with Solomon and had access to his other scholarly teachers. She sometimes received special instructions from him (1 Kings 10: 4-5).

After observing Solomon's outstanding daily behavior and leadership abilities, the queen provided him with a personal report (1 Kings 10: 6-7). Makeda's training covered religious matters and other subjects coming from Solomon and his high-ranking leaders (1 Kings

## CHALLENGING QUESTION

How could the Ethiopian empire develop large commercial trade programs with countries like Israel and be virtually ignored in traditional Bible teachings?

10:9). The wealth and commercial trading practices of the Ethiopians are exhibited again as 1 Kings 10:10 mentioned the enormous amount of gold and abundant supply of regular and special spices Makeda gave to Solomon earlier in 1 Kings 10:2.

First Kings 10:11 introduces the Phoenician king Hiram. The Phoenicians were descendants from Canaanite ancestry, meaning they also were from Ham's family tree. Hiram maintained a navy for his nation of people, in addition to high-level commercial trade and commerce. Note that this story features two descendants from Ham's family tree — an Ethiopian (Makeda) and a Phoenician (Hiram). Chapter 11 will review Hiram's role in helping Solomon in building the Temple in Jerusalem.

While 1 Kings 10:13 ends the passage, Makeda's legacy has burned bright in biblical and historical accounts for the past 3,000 years. Very few historical figures can match her longevity or greatness to enduring fame.

## CHALLENGING QUESTION

We see the interaction between ancient black- and brown-skinned nations working together in the Old Testament scriptures. Why does modern history overlook or minimize these key biblical events involving these powerful black nations?

## Makeda's Legacy

Near the end of her visit, Solomon made romantic advances on the young queen and she rebuked his attempts. Later, he tried again and was able to win Makeda's favor; she became pregnant with their child. She returned to her homeland with a biracial son (part-Israelite and part-Ethiopian) named Menelik. After her reign, Menelik became a well-known ruler of the Ethiopian empire.

The ancestral lineage from Makeda through Menelik continued down to 20$^{th}$-century Ethiopian ruler Haile Selassie — more than 3,000 plus years of continuous genealogy records of Makeda's royal bloodlines.

## Yemen's Claims

The country of Yemen also claims the Queen of Sheba's heritage as belonging to their ancestry. According to the Yemeni version, the Queen of Sheba was called "Bilquis" and ruled over an ancient kingdom in present-day Yemen. A region called Saba existed in Yemen during this period, and some historians think that the names "Saba" and "Sheba" are connected.

Interestingly, there are three descendants listed under Noah's family tree for Noah's son Ham, named Sheba, Seba and Sabath. There is also one descendant listed under Noah's son Shem named Sheba (see Noah's family genealogical tree on Page 23). There also exists old folklore stories that the Yemen region could have been part of the Ethiopian empire in ancient times.

In summary, after years of research and reviewing both versions of the stories for the Queen of Sheba, this book respectfully accepts the Kebra Nagast versions of Ethiopian history for Queen Makeda.

## Summary

No other queen in the Bible had the impactful historical references as the ones made of Queen Makeda. In addition to her Old Testament stories, the fact that Jesus made direct quotes about this queen in Matthew 12:42 almost 1,000 years after her death shows the long-term biblical impact that she had on the people of Israel.

## TALKING POINTS

Ethiopia's society was so advanced that it often chose female rulers who led the empire to world prominence. This unique cultural shift contrasted with the traditional patriarchal rulers in other Old Testament nations. In addition to the Queen of Sheba and Queen Candace's biblical listings, Ethiopia had eight female rulers of the ancient Cushite (Ethiopian) empire called the Candace queens, who ruled before and after the birth of Jesus.

1.) What do you think about the Ethiopians choosing female queens to rule their empire instead of the traditional male leaders?

2.) What are your thoughts on two of the more powerful biblical queens being Ethiopian ancestry — Queen Makeda (the Queen of Sheba) and Queen Candace?

3.) Why was Queen Makeda the only queen to make the Old Testament, New Testament and the Qur'an?

# 6

# Ebedmelech, the Ethiopian Servant

*"A people will never look forward to posterity who never look backward to their ancestors."*

**Edmund Burke**[41]

## OBJECTIVE

Throughout the Old Testament, the Ethiopians appear in stories in positions of leadership, prominence and influence. In this chapter, the Ethiopian servant Ebedmelech used his special skills to save the life of Jeremiah, one of the major prophets in the Bible.

Ebedmelech was an Ethiopian servant to the Israelite King Zedekiah of Judah. Ebedmelech's story starts in Jeremiah 38:1-13 when Jeremiah, one of the major prophets of the Old Testament around 627 B.C., received a calling to warn the people of Jerusalem of pending destruction of their city by the Babylonians.

Jeremiah told Zedekiah and the Israelites that they were disobedient to God's laws. After listening to Jeremiah's predictions, Zedekiah held

41. Rogers, J.A. World's Great Men of Color. Vol. 1 (1972). New York, NY: McMillan Publishing. Page 1.

a meeting with important officials from his kingdom. After much discussion, the king decided to hand Jeremiah over to a group of Israelite leaders who wanted to kill him. These men later placed Jeremiah in a dungeon to die.

Ebedmelech was working as a servant in Jerusalem, which was a long way from his homeland of Ethiopia. He was multilingual as he communicated to Zedekiah in the king's native language. Ebedmelech was respected enough to hold a position in the king's court and held enough influence that he could persuade Zedekiah to change his decision and spare Jeremiah's life. Ebedmelech skillfully intervened as he went before Zedekiah and spoke compassionately with a plea to spare Jeremiah's life.

## CHALLENGING QUESTION

How did an Ethiopian rise to such prominence in Zedekiah's court to where he could speak freely to influence the king's decisions?

After persuading Zedekiah to release Jeremiah, Ebedmelech took a group of men and rescued Jeremiah from the dungeon: According to Jeremiah 38: 10-13, Ebedmelech assumed the leadership role among the 30 men who rescued Jeremiah.

In Jeremiah 39: 15-18, God honored the faithful work of Ebedmelech and God said he would spare the servant when the Babylonians came to destroy Jerusalem. God recognized this Ethiopian man's service and obedience and blessed him. Even though Ebedmelech was not an Israelite, God showed him special favor:

> *15 "Now the word of the Lord came unto Jeremiah, while he was shut up in the court of the prison, saying,*
>
> *16 "'Go and speak to Ebedmelech the Ethiopian, saying, 'Thus saith the Lord of hosts, the God of Israel;*

*Behold, I will bring my words upon this city for evil, and not for good; and they shall be accomplished in that day before thee.*

*17 "'But I will deliver thee in that day, saith the Lord; and thou shalt not be given into the hand of men of whom thou art afraid.*

*18 "'For I will surely deliver thee, and thou shalt not fall by the sword, but thy life shall be for a prey unto thee: because thou hast put thy trust in me,' saith the Lord."*

**Jeremiah 39:15-18**

**CHALLENGING QUESTION**

These scriptures show another example of the unique relationship between Old Testament writers and the Ethiopians. Why have modern biblical scholars not emphasized this bond more in teachings?

## Summary

Ebedmelech — an Ethiopian man, which makes him a descendant of Ham — saved Jeremiah's life by displaying wisdom, diplomacy and bravery to Israelite King Zedekiah. Moreover, Ebedmelech demonstrates a continual pattern of Ethiopians playing influential roles throughout the Old Testament, which contradicts the notion there was no black presence in the Bible.

## TALKING POINTS

Ebedmelech was an Ethiopian servant to the Israelite King Zedekiah of Judah. His story shows another Ethiopian in a unique situation in the Old Testament; in his story, his influence saved the prophet Jeremiah from death.

1.) Why did Ebedmelech's persuasive appeal to save Jeremiah's life overrule all of the king's special court adviser's opinions?

2.) Why would a humble servant — a non-Israelite, a foreigner from Ethiopian lands — gain such powerful influence in the Israelite king's court?

# 7

# The Land of Canaan

*"Because the real history of mankind is not a part of our general knowledge, we are discounting factors most needed to secure world balance."*

**Drusilla Dunjee Houston**[42]

## OBJECTIVE

This chapter will challenge the unfounded myths and opinions that have portrayed Canaan and the Canaanite people in a negative light. Discussions will center around the healthy and vibrant Hamite culture that existed in these biblical lands.

Little information, outside of biblical scriptures, was known about ancient Canaanite people until the 20th century. In the Old Testament, the lands of Canaan and the Canaanite people are one of the most talked-about subjects of that era. The Old Testament mentions Canaan and the Canaanites more than 70 times each.

This chapter will review Canaan in the following topics:

- Canaan, the biblical person, who was the founder and ancestor to the Canaanite nation.

42. Houston, Drusilla Dunjee (1985). Wonderful Ethiopians of the Ancient Cushite Empire. Baltimore, MD: Black Classics Press. Pages 11-12.

- The lands of Canaan, which focuses on the original people and the later migrations that led to the mixing among people.
- The region's geography.
- The Canaanite people before the Israelite conquest.
- The Canaanite people after the Israelite conquest.

## Canaan, the Person

Genesis 10 described Canaan, the son of Ham and the grandson of Noah, as the founder of the biblical nation named after him. Canaan was a biblical member of the Hamite nations, as were his Old Testament-era descendants. In Genesis 10:6, Canaan along with his brothers are listed as the four sons of Ham:

> *"And the sons of Ham; Cush, and Mizraim, and Phut, and Canaan."*
>
> **Genesis 10:6**

Modern historians and skeptics have downplayed the biblical writings on Canaan's ethnic identity. The Old Testament scriptures did not describe Canaan as belonging to the white nations (Japhetites) or brown Asiatic nations (Semites).

Genesis 9 and 10 singled out Canaan by making sure to document that he was unmistakably the son of Ham. There are three distinct verses in Genesis that highlight Canaan's genealogy and tie him directly to Ham and the black nations — Genesis 10:6, Genesis 9:18 and Genesis 9:22 (Note: None of Ham's other three sons received similar quotes):

> *"And the sons of Noah, that went forth of the ark, were Shem, and Ham, and Japheth: and Ham is the father of Canaan."*
>
> **Genesis 9:18**

> *"And Ham, the father of Canaan, saw the nakedness of his father, and told his two brethren without."*
>
> **Genesis 9:22**

*"And the sons of Ham; Cush, and Mizraim, and Phut, and Canaan."*

**Genesis 10:6**

**CHALLENGING QUESTION**

Why did the Old Testament writers make such an effort to make the connection between Canaan and his father, Ham?

Genesis 10:15-19 are five genealogy verses dedicated to Canaan, his lands and his descendants. Notably, one grandson of Noah was given significant coverage within the 30 specific genealogy verses concerning the repopulation of the earth after the Great Flood:

*15 "And Canaan begat Sidon his firstborn, and Heth,*

*16 "And the Jebusite, and the Amorite, and the Girgasite,*

*17 "And the Hivite, and the Arkite, and the Sinite,*

*18 "And the Arvadite, and the Zemarite, and the Hamathite: and afterward were the families of the Canaanites spread abroad.*

*19 "And the border of the Canaanites was from Sidon, as thou comest to Gerar, unto Gaza; as thou goest, unto Sodom, and Gomorrah, and Admah, and Zeboim, even unto Lasha."*

**Genesis 10:15-19**

Canaan received more genealogy verses than Noah's son Japheth, the father of the white nations who received only four verses (Genesis 10: 2-5).

## The Original Canaanites and Their Lands

The Old Testament writers portrayed the Canaanites as the adversaries to the main heroes of the Bible, the Israelites. This limited view gave an incomplete picture of the real prominence of the

**DID YOU KNOW?**

Canaanite descendants also include the Hittites, Philistines, Phoenicians and Sidonians.

Canaanites. This chapter will examine the Canaanites' history to get a better understanding of their actual legacy.

Genesis 10:19 describes the Canaan lands and boundaries, which include present-day Israel, Lebanon, parts of Syria and parts of western Jordan. Ancient prominent Canaanite cites included Tyre, Sidon, Jericho and Gaza, Ugarit, Biblos, Megiddo and Jebus (the original name for Jerusalem) (see map).

Canaanite people were represented throughout the Old Testament in stories, human migrations and human strife. The Canaanites were a federation of loosely maintained city-states that worked independently, even though they belonged to the overall region of Canaan. This loose confederation also prohibited the Canaanites from uniting during critical invasions and warfare times for the total protection of their lands.

The Old Testament uses the term "Canaanite" as a general description of the people in the region. However, the descendants of Canaan listed in Genesis 10 also used their subgroup names to identify themselves. These descendants included the Amorites, Arkites, Arvadites, Girgasites, Hamathites, Hittites, Hivites, Jebusites, Philistines, Phoenicians, Sidonians, Sinites and Zemarites.

## Major Archaeological Discovery

Until the 20th century, the primary source of information available to the western world about the Canaanites were the writings contained in the Old Testament. Without biblical writings and stories, the world might have overlooked the overall Canaanite legacy.

Unfortunately, the centuries-old reliance on the Bible helped shape the negative biases, beliefs and opinions of the Canaanites.

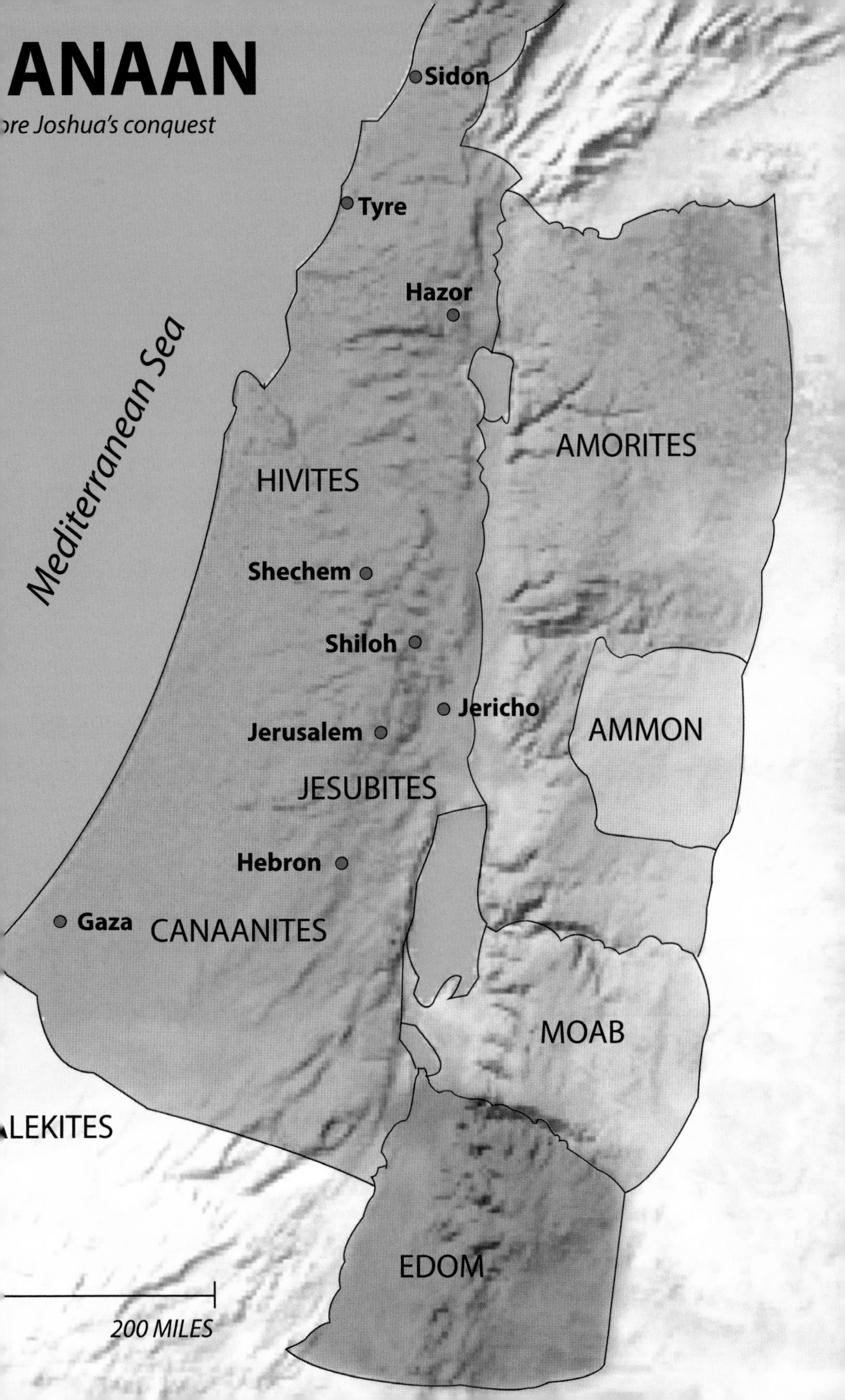

ANAAN
ore Joshua's conquest
Sidon
Tyre
Hazor
Mediterranean Sea
AMORITES
HIVITES
Shechem
Shiloh
Jericho
Jerusalem
AMMON
JESUBITES
Hebron
Gaza
CANAANITES
MOAB
LEKITES
EDOM
200 MILES

SHUTTERSTOCK
**Ugarit was an ancient port city in northern Syria. In 1928, a farmer discovered an extensive cemetery. Its ruins are often called Ras Shamra after the region where they lie.**

The Bible did not tell the full story about their backgrounds and their history. However, a lot of these historical views changed when a great archeology discovery took place in 1928 when a farmer discovered an extensive cemetery in the Ugarit region of Syria.

SHUTTERSTOCK
**The Baal Cycle of the Ugaritic texts on display in the Louvre in Paris.**

Shortly after the discovery, excavations began in the region and the nearby area (called Ras Sharma) and lasted for nearly 50 years. Ugarit contained the remains of Canaanite temples, house dwellings and work areas. The discoveries also uncovered temples dedicated to the Canaanite gods Baal and El.

However, the most important discoveries were the clay tablets that contained religious and mythology stories of the

Canaanites' spiritual beliefs. These cuneiform clay tablets date back to 1200 B.C. Some tablets were in better physical shape than others that were broken and needed special handling.

The vast collection of clay tablets and other artifacts provided a better picture of the Canaanites' religion. The tablets also offered a deeper understanding and recognition of the extent and influence of the Canaanite civilization during ancient times.

## Canaanite Religion and Baal

Part of the overall Canaanite cultural influence was their religious practices of worshipping multiple gods. Included in the pantheon or grouping of Canaanite gods were El, Baal, Dagan and Mot; the goddesses were Anat and Asherah. The head of the gods was El, but Baal was the most prominent god among the Canaanites.

Baal was a known god to the Canaanites more than 1,000 years before Abraham and the Hebrew people existed. The Canaanite people believed that Baal was the ruler of their people and their universe.

As the god of fertility, rain and weather, Baal was highly visible and passionately worshipped among Canaanite people. The Canaanite lands were in hot and dry regions that suffered severe droughts, so the Canaanite worshippers depended on Baal to provide the needed rains.

Baal also had a profound effect on the Semite people, including the Hebrews of the Old Testament, who acknowledged and often worshipped him. The Old Testament made approximately 80 references to Baal. In several instances, the scriptures refer to Baal as "lord" or "master." The following citings refer to Baal under the following names:

- Baal-gad (lord of good fortune) — Joshua 11:17
- Baal-hamon (lord of wealth) — Song of Solomon 8:11
- Baal-Hazor (Baal's village) — 2 Samuel 13:23

- Baal-meon (lord of the dwelling) — Numbers 32:38
- Baal-peor (lord of the opening)— Deuteronomy 4:3
- Baal-tamar (lord of the tree) — Judges 20:33
- Baal-perazim (lord of the breakthroughs) — 2 Samuel 5:20
- Baal-Berith (lord of the covenant) — Judges 8:33

The Old Testament contains scriptures that use other variations of his name in forms such as Baalim, Baale, Baalperazim, EshBaal, Meribaal, Beeliada and Beel.

The visibility of Baal's impact on people of the Old Testament era was evident in the references as mentioned earlier. From a historical perspective, Baal significantly influenced people's lives and his relevance in the Canaanite culture is too prominent to dismiss.

**CHALLENGING QUESTION**

Why would a pagan god gather constant references and so much attention within the Old Testament?

## Language and Ethnic Identification

Bias and misinformation in research on ancient history have created generally accepted theories that do not align with facts or logic. Many modern history books contradict what ancient historians and writers wrote about ancient black nations.

The Canaanites are a prime example of modern historians creating information that disagrees with ancient history. Genesis 10 states that the Canaanites are the descendants of Ham's son, Canaan. The entire genealogy of Canaan's people are listed as Hamites, meaning they are part of Ham's family tree. There is no mention of the Canaanites belonging to the family trees of Noah's other sons, Shem and Japheth.

However, modern historians have found ways to classify a lot of the

Canaanites as Semites. They have done this through the "language spoken" concept by certain ancient nations, saying that the language spoken identifies the ethnic origin of the people themselves.

An example comes from Steve Wyrick, professor of religion at the University of Mary Hardin-Baylor, and his valuable writing on this subject. Included in his writing is a definition for a Semite, which illustrates some modern-day thinking:

> *"A person who claims descent from Noah's son Shem (Genesis 5:32, 10:21-31) or more precisely as a linguistic term, those people speaking one of the Semitic languages."*[43]

The first Semite definition — the person is a descendant of Noah's son, Shem — is consistent with the Old Testament information. The second part of the description — classifying a Semite solely on speaking a type of Semitic language — is not found in the Old Testament.

Modern scholars have decided to reclassify many Hamite nations from Ham to Shem, primarily based on the concept of "language spoken." Among the Hamites that scholars reclassified as Semites include the Akkadians and ancient Babylonians in Mesopotamia, the Canaanites and the Phoenicians. Wyrick references this thought with the following quote:

> *"The racial list in Genesis and the list of linguists do not always include the same people groups. The place of origin for the Semites is difficult to determine."*[44]

Wyrick acknowledged there is a disagreement between Old Testament definitions of nations and the modern-day reclassifying of biblical nations. In the second part, there is an admission that "the place of origin for the Semites is difficult to determine."

In contrast, there is no debate regarding the Hamite nations being at the beginning of civilization; their existence is noted in Genesis

43. Brand, Chad; Draper, Charles; England, Archie (2003). Holman Illustrated Bible Dictionary. Nashville, TN: Holman Bible Publishers. Page 1461.

44. Ibid., Page 1461.

in nations such as Ethiopia, Egypt and ancient Mesopotamia and supported by external history records.

Genesis 10 cites Nimrod — Ham's grandson— as the founder of the Mesopotamian region known as the Fertile Crescent. In Genesis 10, all groupings of Canaanites, Phoenicians, ancient Babylonians (see Chapter Four) and Akkadians (see Chapter Four) are listed as descendants of Ham. The Egyptians and Ethiopians also belong to Ham's family tree.

Yet influential reference books have tied the language spoken to the ethnic origin of these people and moved them from Ham's family tree and placed them under Shem's, such as this passage from Wyrick:

> *"Three major divisions exist in the Semitic family of languages, East Semitic would include Akkadian used in ancient Babylon and Assyria. Northwest Semitic involves Hebrew, Aramic, Syrian, Phoenician, Samaritan, Canaanite, Moabite. South Semitic includes Arabic, Sabean, Minean, Ethiopic. Approximately 70 distinct forms of Semitic languages are known."*[45]

In essence, the above quote includes Hamite nations defined in Genesis 10 — such as the Canaanites, Ethiopians, Phoenicians and Sabeans — as reclassified as Semite people.

Looking at the language spoken and directly tying the people's ethnic origin solely based on language is flawed. Modern-day examples of languages spoken by people versus their actual ethnic origin include:

- Black people who live in France and speak French, but their racial origins are still of African descent.
- Black people who live in Germany and speak German, but their racial origins are still of African descent.

45. Brand, Chad; Draper, Charles; England, Archie (2003). Holman Illustrated Bible Dictionary. Nashville, TN: Holman Bible Publishers. Page 1461.

- Black people who live in England and speak English, but their racial origins are still of African descent.
- Black people who live in the United States and speak English, but their racial origins are still of African descent.

Even if the Canaanites did use a Semitic language at some time, it still does not minimize the fact that Genesis 10 cites the Canaanites as a black nation.

Perhaps this modern-day theory of reclassifying people was a systematic way of reducing the presence of the biblical black nations and making them disappear from the Bible, but this "language spoken" identification process contradicts the Old Testament Genesis 10 documented records.

**DID YOU KNOW?**

When reviewing the old Hebrew language, Thomas Smothers, professor of Old Testament and Hebrew at the Southern Baptist Theological Seminary, references that the old Hebrew language was connected to the ancient Canaanite dialects and similar to the Phoenician language.[46]

Historian H.G. Wells stated that the Hamitic language was used more than either Semitic or Aryan languages in ancient days.[47]

Author Drucilla Dunjee Houston said that the more recent language in Babylonian times was Semitic, but the inscriptions on buildings in the more ancient times of Chaldea showed they were Hamitic.[48]

Finally, George Rawlinson said the ancient ruins of Chaldea were Cushite, and the language found among the ruins was not the Semitic

46. Brand, Chad; Draper, Charles; England, Archie (2003). Holman Illustrated Bible Dictionary. Nashville, TN: Holman Bible Publishers. Pages 735-736.
47. Houston, Drusilla Dunjee (1985). Wonderful Ethiopians of the Ancient Cushite Empire. Baltimore, MD: Black Classics Press. Page 17.
48. Ibid., Page 162.

language of the more recent Assyrian Empire.[49]

In summary, the ancient Canaanite people were Hamites and not Semites.

**CHALLENGING QUESTION**

Why would the early Hebrews live among the Canaanites, whom the Old Testament writers called pagans and heathens?

## Canaan before the Israelite Conquest

Canaan's biblical prominence started in Genesis with the story of Abraham and his travels to this country. The Canaanite nation was well established by 3000 B.C. However, the earliest inhabitants of the region were in the city of Jericho, going as far back as 8000 B.C. In contrast, Abraham, who is considered the father of the Hebrew and Israelite nation, lived around 1900 B.C.

The Hebrew leaders Abraham, Isaac, Jacob and Joseph all lived in Canaan during their lifetimes. These early Hebrew people lived among the Canaanite people and enjoyed the favorable climate, agriculture and prosperous conditions within the lands.

**DID YOU KNOW?**

The ancient city Jebus, cited in Judges 19:10, was the capital of the Jebusites, a Canaanite tribe (for genealogy, see Genesis 10:16). David conquered the Jebusites and renamed their city from Jebus to Jerusalem (2 Samuel 5:6-10).

49. Houston, Drusilla Dunjee (1985). Wonderful Ethiopians of the Ancient Cushite Empire. Baltimore, MD: Black Classics Press. Pages 164-165.

| CITY | ORIGINAL OLD TESTAMENT ERA INHABITANTS | APPROXIMATE DATE OF FIRST INHABITANTS * |
|---|---|---|
| Jericho | Canaanites | 8000 B.C. |
| Byblos (Gebal) | Canaanites | 8000 B.C. |
| Megiddo | Canaanites | 7000 B.C. |
| Ugarit | Canaanites | 6500 B.C. |
| Ashkelon | Canaanites | 5880 B.C. |
| Hebron | Canaanites | 3300 B.C. |
| Tyre | Canaanites | 2000 B.C. |

*__NOTE__: Earliest Inhabitants Approximate Date indicates the archaeologist and excavation records on the earliest signs of human occupation in these cities. These ancient dates could involve ancient Cushite or Anu people. These cities are ancient and do not have Semite or Japhetite beginnings.

## Canaan's Economic Prowess

Canaanite people were highly skilled business and commercial traders during the Old Testament era. The geographic location allowed them to serve as a connection between Mesopotamia, Egypt, Ethiopia and the Mediterranean Sea.

While the Israelites were in captivity in Egypt for 400 years, Canaan flourished in its ability to import and export goods from countries as they skillfully traveled throughout the Mediterranean Sea. An example of Canaan's prowess and culture was the city of Ugarit, which dates back to at least 4000 B.C. Ugarit was located along the major trade routes connecting Mesopotamia and Egypt, and possessed a harbor that could serve boats involved in commercial trade.

Canaanite cities were advanced and progressive with well-maintained buildings. They created farming and agriculture systems capable of sustaining large populations. The Canaanites were not waiting on Israelites for culture, knowledge or development of civilization. While the two groups shared distinctly different religious views, these differences did not mean that the Canaanites were subordinate to the Israelites.

The Canaanites are interwoven into the fabric of the Old Testament. Characters such as Rahab of Jericho, Judah's daughter-in-law Tamar, King Hiram of Sidon and Judah's wife Shuah were Canaanites. The Old Testament might seem incomplete if Canaanite culture and stories were removed.

Canaan's loose confederation of city-states led to its decline and worked against the region when outside forces came to conquer their lands. During the Old Testament, Egypt gained periodic control over portions of their commercial trading routes. Later, when the Israelites came to conquer the area, the Canaanites made little attempts to produce a stable, unified regional defense.

**CHALLENGING QUESTION**

Why is there an ongoing negative perception of the Canaanites and their civilization?

## Canaan after the Israelite Invasion

After their deliverance from slavery in Egypt, the Israelites received instructions from God that they would receive Canaan as their new homeland._

However, one of the challenges facing the Israelites was how to engage with the various groups of people already living in Canaan. This conflict resulted in numerous battles as the Israelites attempted to conquer the Canaanite people.

Deuteronomy 20:16-17 and Joshua 3:10 contained verses on the Israelites' planned genocidal practices against the Canaanites:

> *"But of the cities of these people, which the LORD thy God doth give thee for an inheritance, thou shalt save alive nothing that breatheth:*

*"But thou shalt utterly destroy them; namely, the Hittites, and the Amorites, the Canaanites, and the Perizzites, the Hivites, and the Jebusites; as the LORD thy God hath commanded thee."*

**Deuteronomy 20:16-17**

*"And Joshua said, Hereby ye shall know that the living God is among you, and that he will without fail drive out from before you the Canaanites, and the Hittites, and the Hivites, and the Perizzites, and the Girgashites, and the Amorites, and the Jebusites."*

**Joshua 3:10**

There is an ongoing debate among biblical scholars on whether God instructed the Israelites to carry out these disturbing genocidal deeds. However, the second part of the discussion is whether the Israelites were successful in eliminating all Canaanites.

From a historical perspective, the Israelites never accomplished its goal of eliminating the Canaanites. The Old Testament does not state anywhere that the Israelites eliminated or drove the Canaanites out of the region. Even though they suffered military defeats and surrendered some territories, the Canaanites did not leave their homelands.

The Canaanite people remained in their lands and the cities which they had built. The Books of Joshua and Judges provide recorded scriptures that state the Israelites lived among the Canaanite people in the same cities and communities long after the Israelite conquest.

Joshua 24:13 describes how the Israelites came into Canaan and settled in existing cities which they did not build. The Bible showed a pattern of the Israelites moving into the developed Canaanite cities. However, there was no pattern of Canaanites moving into Israelite cities.

*"And I have given you a land for which ye did not labour, and cities which ye built not, and ye dwell in them; of the vineyards and oliveyards which ye planted not do ye eat."*

**Joshua 24:13**

Initially, the Israelites and Canaanites lived together as neighbors who often married each other and produced a multitude of biracial children. Joshua 17:16 and 18 stated the Canaanites lived in the mountainous regions and had chariots in their strong military.

The possession of chariots showed military strength and organization during these ancient times. The Canaanites had chariots while the Israelites did not possess this level of military equipment. The Canaanites were familiar with iron and how to use it constructively in their military and overall lifestyles.

> *16 "And the children of Joseph said, The hill is not enough for us: and all the Canaanites that dwell in the land of the valley have chariots of iron, both they who are of Bethshean and her towns, and they who are of the valley of Jezreel.*
>
> *18 "But the mountain shall be thine; for it is a wood, and thou shalt cut it down: and the outgoings of it shall be thine: for thou shalt drive out the Canaanites, though they have iron chariots, and though they be strong."*
>
> **Joshua 17:16-18**

Judges 1:19 talks about the tribe of Judah's battle encounters with the Canaanites. The Israelites were unable to defeat them and listed the Canaanites as having chariots within their military:

> *"And the LORD was with Judah; and he drove out the inhabitants of the mountain; but could not drive out the inhabitants of the valley, because they had chariots of iron."*
>
> **Judges 1:19**

## Living Together in Canaan

After the Israelite conquest and occupation, the Bible documented that the two groups lived among each other in many regions of Canaan lands. Joshua 16:10 and Joshua 17:12 showed how the Israelites lived among the Canaanites:

SHUTTERSTOCK
**A gold bowl found in Ugarit depicting a Canaanite warrior in a chariot.**

> *"And they drave not out the Canaanites that dwelt in Gezer: but the Canaanites dwell among the Ephraimites unto this day, and serve under tribute."*
>
> **Joshua 16:10**

> *"Yet the children of Manasseh could not drive out the inhabitants of those cities; but the Canaanites would dwell in that land."*
>
> **Joshua 17:12**

Judges 1:27-33 described various places in Canaan where the Israelites and Canaanites lived together. More specifically, some of the leaders of the 12 Tribes of Israel — Asher, Ephraim, Manasseh, Naphtali and Zebulun — were not able to drive the Canaanites away from their homelands and lived together in the Canaanite cities.

## Living Together and Intermixing

Judges 3:1-6 provided an overview of God's directive for the Israelites to dwell among the Canaanites. These verses identified many Canaanite groups by their biblical names. Judges 3:5-6 are relevant because they spoke directly to the continual intermixing and marriages, as Israelite men married Canaanite women and Canaanite men married Israelite women:

> *"And the children of Israel dwelt among the Canaanites, Hittites, and Amorites, and Perizzites, and Hivites, and Jebusites:*
>
> *"And they took their daughters to be their wives, and gave their daughters to their sons, and served their gods."*
>
> **Judges 3:5,6**

The early Israelites were connected to Canaanite culture through marriages, children and by living in the same cities. This union produced a noticeable mixture of people with dual ancestry from both groups. Children from the biblically mentioned patriarch Israelite (father) and Canaanite (mother) mixed marriages, would be included among the early Israelites.

## King Jabin, Canaanite Ruler

In Judges 4:1-3, there was an unusual story involving the Israelites and Canaanites. During this period, the Israelites began their conquest of Canaan and had fought many battles with the inhabitants. Later, the Israelites began living in Canaanite cities and dwelling among the residents.

The Bible mentioned that King Jabin and his Canaanite people lived in certain northern regions. These Canaanites were not under the control of the new Israelite settlers. This story contradicts the beliefs that the invading Israelites conquered and eliminated all Canaanites from their homelands:

> *1 "And the children of Israel again did evil in the sight of the LORD, when Ehud was dead."*
>
> *2 "And the LORD sold them into the hand of Jabin king of Canaan, that reigned in Hazor; the captain of whose host was Sisera, which dwelt in Harosheth of the Gentiles."*
>
> *3 "And the children of Israel cried unto the LORD: for he*

> *had nine hundred chariots of iron; and twenty years he mightily oppressed the children of Israel."*
>
> **Judges 4:1-3**

Judges 4:2 tells that Jabin reigned over the ancient city of Hazor in the northern regions of Canaan. Hazor was considered an important commercial city in ancient times. The passage also states that God sold the Israelites into bondage to Jabin and the Canaanites.

The first part of Judges 4:3 states the Canaanites possessed 900 military chariots constructed with iron. As previously mentioned, the Canaanites were already using iron and iron-related products when the Israelites were still trying to find the basic principles of civilization. The second part of this verse shows God allowed Jabin to oppress the Israelites for 20 years. Whether it was through direct servitude or other forms of subordination, the critical part of this verse is the culturally advanced Canaanites, at one point, were in control of the Israelites.

**CHALLENGING QUESTION**

How do you explain King Jabin's rule over the Israelites if the Canaanites were supposedly backward and heathen people?

## The Color Purple

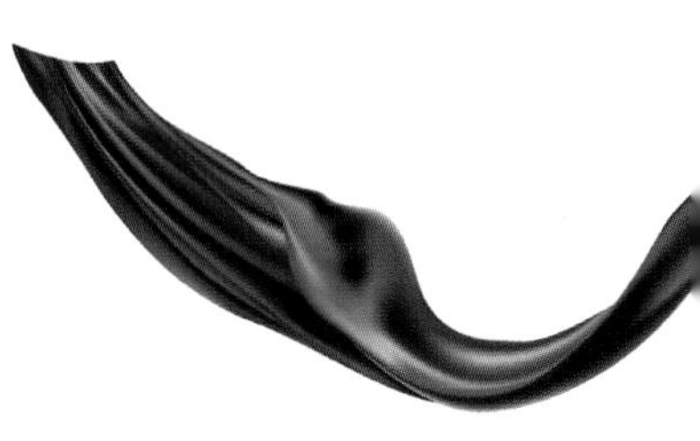

The Canaanites developed the process for extracting the purple dye from soft shell animals called mollusk. They transferred the dye into a purple-colored cloth, which became a prestigious symbol. The Canaanites sold the material to neighboring countries and royal families and wealthy people usually wore the cloth. The high demands of purple fabric from other nations added substantial wealth to Canaanite people.

## The Phoenicians

The Canaanites' descendants, the Phoenicians, lived among the northern regions of the old Canaan lands that would include parts of present-day Lebanon. Their timeline spanned from approximately 2000 B.C. until 500 B.C.

The Phoenicians were highly-skilled sea travelers and merchants whose skills of transporting and trading in goods and luxury items were widely respected. They regularly sailed throughout the Mediterranean Sea and established regional trading ports and commercial stations. Additionally, they used a reliable system of weights and measurements for conducting business transactions.

**PHOENICIAN ALPHABET**

*Comparison with the modern alphabet*

| | | | |
|---|---|---|---|
| A | 𐤀 | P | 𐤐 |
| B | 𐤁 | Q | 𐤒 |
| D | 𐤃 | R | 𐤓 |
| G | 𐤂 | S | 𐤔 |
| H | 𐤄 | S | 𐤑 |
| H | 𐤇 | S | 𐤎 |
| K | 𐤊 | T | 𐤕 |
| L | 𐤋 | T | 𐤈 |
| M | 𐤌 | W | 𐤅 |
| N | 𐤍 | Y | 𐤉 |
| O | 𐤏 | Z | 𐤆 |

**NOTE:** The Phoenician alphabet did not include vowels. After the Phoenicians passed their alphabet system to the Greeks, the Greeks added the five vowels.

## The Alphabet

The Canaanites developed and later passed the alphabet system to the Phoenicians. The Phoenicians, during their business interactions, shared the alphabet writing with an emerging group of people called the Greeks around the eighth century B.C. The Greeks later took this alphabet system, made limited changes and subsequently passed the Phoenician-based alphabet throughout Europe. This alphabet system is used around the world and traces its roots to the Phoenician alphabet.

## Summary

The Canaanites' legacy and impact on both ancient and modern civilizations are noteworthy. Their history is full of achievements and contributions to the overall advancement of humanity. The Bible provided recorded evidence that the early Israelites included some people of Canaanite ancestry. During the Old Testament era, it was common for some people to have both Hamite and Semite bloodlines in their ancestry.

### TALKING POINTS

The Canaanites are arguably the most misunderstood people in the Old Testament. This chapter shows that the Canaanites were a stable, advanced and progressive civilization. Hebrew leaders such as Abraham, Isaac, Jacob and Judah lived and prospered in Canaan, not in Semite-based nations. When the Israelites invaded Canaan, the Israelites moved into well-established Canaanite cities. The Canaanite civilization goes back to at least 3000 B.C., which is much older than Abraham and the Hebrew people.

1.) Why are Canaanite people so misunderstood in the Old Testament? What would be the historical-biblical impacts of providing complete and well-rounded information on the real legacies of the Canaanites?

2.) Why didn't the Israelites stop interfacing, marrying and socially connecting with the Canaanite people?

3.) Why do you think so many of Ham's Canaanite descendants in Genesis 10 were later switched in modern history to become members of the Semite and Japhetite nations?

# Semite Leaders

# Abraham

*"Neither shall thy name any more be called Abram, but thy name shall be Abraham; for a father of many nations have I made thee."*

**Genesis 17:5**

**OBJECTIVE**

This chapter reviews the historical significance of the Hamite nations in Abraham's life. Having lived his entire life in Hamite lands, Abraham displayed an unusually high dependence on these black nations.

The next four chapters will look at the lives of biblical leaders Abraham, Joseph, Judah, Moses and Solomon. Each had notable interaction with black nations through travels, living among the people and marrying Hamite women.

Abraham is the common patriarch of Judaism, Christianity and Islam, but he also is a central figure of the Hebrew people. Abraham lived around 1900 B.C. and received a calling to start a journey from his homeland in Chaldea to live in Canaan. Abraham's original name was Abram (meaning "father is exalted"). His name was later changed to Abraham (meaning "father of the multitude"), as explained in Genesis 17:5.

Abraham was a descendant from Shem, making Abraham a Semite and not a member of the genealogy from Noah's sons Japheth and Ham. Genesis 11:10-26 explains Abraham's genealogy, starting with Shem and culminating in Genesis 11:26 with Abraham's father, Terah:

> *"And Terah lived seventy years, and begat Abram, Nahor, and Haran."*
>
> **Genesis 11:26**

Genesis 11 begins Abraham's story and names his homeland as Ur in the land of Chaldea (Genesis 11:31). Ur was part of the Mesopotamian region that the Cushite, Nimrod, founded:

> *"And Terah took Abram his son, and Lot the son of Haran his son's son, and Sarai his daughter-in-law, his son Abram's wife; and they went forth with them from Ur of the Chaldees, to go into the land of Canaan; and they came unto Haran, and dwelt there."*
>
> **Genesis 11:31**

Independent historical research supports the biblical story that the original inhabitants of the Mesopotamian region of Chaldea were Cushites (also referred to as the Ethiopians), as explained in Chapter Four. Historian Drusilla Dunjee Houston stated that "All the earliest traditions of Chaldea center on Nimrod."[50]

Further research from 19th-century historian George Rawlinson concluded that the ruins of Chaldea show Cushite origin, saying the names of Chaldea and Ethiopia "are linked in a way to render any other interpretation impossible."[51]

Abraham was a man who continuously lived among black nations. Genesis 12:5 describes how Abraham left his temporary living quarters in Haran and moved to Canaan, a region inhabited by black people:

> *"And Abram took Sarai his wife, and Lot his brother's son, and all their substance that they had gathered, and*

50. Houston, Drusilla Dunjee (1985). Wonderful Ethiopians of the Ancient Cushite Empire. Baltimore, MD: Black Classics Press. Page 162.
51. Ibid., Pages 164-165.

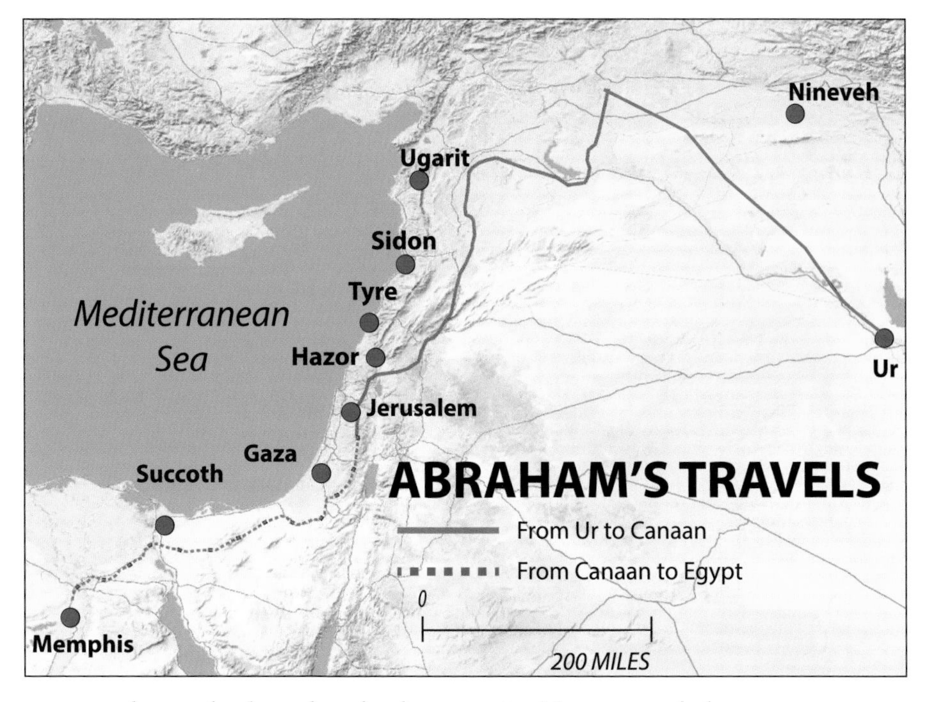


> *the souls that they had gotten in Haran; and they went forth to go into the land of Canaan; and into the land of Canaan they came."*
>
> **Genesis 12:5**

Later on, when famine existed in Canaan lands, Genesis 12:10 says Abraham continued his journey and left Canaan and traveled to Egypt, another black nation:

> *"And there was a famine in the land: and Abram went down into Egypt to sojourn there; for the famine was grievous in the land."*
>
> **Genesis 12:10**

**CHALLENGING QUESTION**

Why didn't Abraham live among the Semite (Asiatic) or Japhetites (white) nations during his early biblical life? Why was Abraham so drawn to the black nations during his early biblical adventures?

During Abraham's time in Canaan, the lands had established a system of healthy regional cities that were prominent and influential. Abraham's travels showed little interaction with the Japhetites. The one place where Abraham would have interacted with all nations of people was at the Tower of Babel, as chronicled in Genesis 11. The Old Testament writers did not record much on Japheth's descendants after the scattering of various nations from the Tower of Babel.

Abraham's story continued with him and his wife Sarai peacefully living in Canaan for 10 years. They both were very old, and Genesis 16:1 and Genesis 16:3 mentioned Sarai could not produce children, so she offered Hagar, their Egyptian maid, to Abraham to bear his children:

> *"Now Sarai Abram's wife bare him no children: and she had a handmaid, an Egyptian, whose name was Hagar."*
>
> **Genesis 16:1**

> *"And Sarai Abram's wife took Hagar her maid the Egyptian, after Abram had dwelt ten years in the land of Canaan, and gave her to her husband Abram to be his wife."*
>
> **Genesis 16:3**

Genesis 16:4 and Genesis 16:15 mentioned that Abraham and Hagar produced a half-Hebrew and half-Egyptian boy named Ishmael:

> *"And he went in unto Hagar, and she conceived: and when she saw that she had conceived, her mistress was despised in her eyes."*
>
> **Genesis 16:4**

> *"And Hagar bare Abram a son: and Abram called his son's name, which Hagar bare, Ishmael."*
>
> **Genesis 16:15**

Genesis 16:16 cites that Abraham was about 86 years old when Ishmael was born. In Genesis 17:15, God changes Sarai's name to Sarah.

Approximately 14 years later in Genesis 21, God blesses Abraham and Sarah with their son, Isaac. However, for historical records, Hagar, a black Egyptian woman, was the mother of Abraham's firstborn son, Ishmael.

## Abraham Buries Sarah in Canaan

Genesis 23 talks about Sarah's death and how Abraham made burial plans, which included purchasing a burial plot in Canaan. This story introduces the Hittites, a group of Canaanite people who were the descendants of Canaan's son Heth (see Genesis 10:15).

The Hittites were part of Ham's genealogy family tree. The Hittites maintained strong cities, and scholars believe they were one of the earliest groups to smelt iron. The original Hittites lived in the Hebron area of the Canaanite lands, which was south of Jerusalem. They also lived in ancient land regions of present-day Turkey. Joshua 1:4 references "all the lands of the Hittites" as being among the northern areas in Canaan:

> *"From the wilderness and this Lebanon even unto the great river, the river Euphrates, all the land of the Hittites, and unto the great sea toward the going down of the sun, shall be your coast."*
>
> **Joshua 1:4**

Some modern-day scholars refer to the Hittites as a Semitic people, while even attempting to tie them to an Indo-European origin. While the Hittites may have mixed with other ethnic groups of people during the Old Testament era, they remained descendants of the black nations from Ham.

Genesis 23:2-7 details how Abraham began searching among the land of Canaan for a proper burial site for Sarah. Abraham does not leave this black nation of people with whom he is deeply acquainted as he makes burial plans for him and Sarah. Abraham shows a great deal of respect for the Hittite people:

> *"'I am a stranger and a sojourner with you: give me a possession of a burying place with you, that I may bury my dead out of my sight."*
>
> **Genesis 23:4**

*"And Abraham stood up, and bowed himself to the people of the land, even to the children of Heth."*

**Genesis 23:7**

## CHALLENGING QUESTION

Why does Abraham show so much respect for the Hittite people by bowing before them in Genesis 23: 7 and Genesis 23:12?

In Genesis 23: 8-20, Abraham met a Hittite man named Ephron and requested to purchase burial land. Abraham negotiated a business deal with Ephron to buy land in the cave of the field of Machpelah, which belonged to the Hittites. Ephron and Abraham completed the real estate-business transaction and Abraham buried Sarah in Canaan, as detailed in the following verses:

*"And he communed with them, saying, 'If it be your mind that I should bury my dead out of my sight; hear me, and entreat for me to Ephron, the son of Zohar."*

**Genesis 23:8**

*"And he spake unto Ephron in the audience of the people of the land, saying, 'But if thou wilt give it, I pray thee, hear me: I will give thee money for the field; take it of me, and I will bury my dead there.'"*

**Genesis 23:13**

*"And after this, Abraham buried Sarah his wife in the cave of the field of Machpelah before Mamre: the same is Hebron in the land of Canaan."*

**Genesis 23:19**

Genesis 25:7-10 stated that when Abraham died, he was buried in the same cave in the field of Machpelah with Sarah.

**CHALLENGING QUESTION**

Why didn't Abraham leave Canaan and bury Sarah in lands belonging to Semite people?

Hundreds of years later, the burial place of Machpelah became the sacred burial grounds for prominent Hebrews Isaac, Rebekah, Leah and Jacob (see Genesis 49:28-33).

**CHALLENGING QUESTION**

Why were the early Hebrew biblical characters Abraham, Sarah, Isaac, Rebekah, Leah and Jacob all buried on Hamite lands instead of Semite lands?

## SUMMARY:

Abraham's life as based on biblical verses:

- Abraham was a member of the Semite race, making him a descendant of Noah's son, Shem.
- Abraham was a Chaldean who came from Ur, part of the Mesopotamia region. The Cushites (descendants of Ham) founded this area.
- Abraham could have possessed some Hamite ancestry. We know about his father, Terah's ancestry, but we do not have detailed information on his mother's lineage.
- Abraham spent a significant portion of his life living in densely populated, Hamite nations.
- Abraham's first child, Ishmael, was born to a black Egyptian woman (Hagar).

- Abraham and Sarai (Sarah) were both buried in the lands of Canaan, home of the ancient black Canaanite nations of people.

Abraham's legacy would be shallow without the constant platform of black nations to support his life's journey. Everywhere he ventured, he was aided by black people who guided him, nurtured him, fed him during a famine and allowed him to grow into the man able to fulfill his life's mission.

## TALKING POINTS

Abraham, the patriarch of the Hebrew people, spent his life living among Hamite nations and Hamite people. He was born in Chaldea (a Mesopotamian region founded by the Cushite Nimrod) and later moved to Canaan for more than 10 years, which included visits to Egypt. Abraham returned to Canaan to spend the rest of his life, where he and his wife were buried. Abraham spent very little of his life in Semite-based nations.

1.) What do you think about Abraham spending his life and being buried among Hamite lands and people (Chaldea and Canaan)?

2.) Why did Abraham decide to be buried in Canaan, per his negotiations with the Hittites in Genesis 23?

# Sons of Jacob

**OBJECTIVE**

This chapter explores Joseph and Judah's marriages to Hamite women and the related impacts on the Twelve Tribes of Israel using a historical lens.

Jacob was a leading figure in the early nation of Israel. He was the son of Isaac and Rebekah, the twin brother of Esau and the grandson of Abraham. Jacob's story covered a large portion of Genesis, starting in Genesis 25 and continuing through Genesis 50. Jacob was the father of 12 sons who became the leaders of the 12 Tribes of Israel.

This chapter will look at Jacob's sons, Joseph and Judah, with an emphasis on their interactions with Hamite people. While they had different mothers (Joseph's mother was Rachel while Judah's mother was Leah), these brothers were the great-grandsons of Abraham.

## Profile of Joseph

> *"And Pharaoh said unto Joseph, 'See, I have set thee over all the land of Egypt.'"*
>
> **Genesis 41:41**

Joseph was the 11th of the 12 sons of Jacob and the youngest child by Jacob's favorite wife, Rachel. Joseph was born in Canaan and was a Semite from the ancestry lines of Noah's son, Shem (Shem -> Arphraxad -> Terah -> Abraham -> Isaac -> Jacob -> Joseph).

Joseph encountered conflicts with his brothers, who were jealous of his favored family status (see Genesis 37). This internal family strife caused his brothers to sell Joseph into slavery, and he eventually ended up in Egypt. Potiphar, an Egyptian captain of Pharaoh's guards, bought Joseph as his servant (Genesis 39:1).

Later based on false accusations by Potiphar's wife, Joseph was put in prison, where he displayed the gift of interpreting dreams. Joseph's special visionary gift allowed him to interpret the Pharaoh's dreams and warn him about an upcoming famine in the land. The Pharaoh rewarded Joseph with the title of the vizier, the second-highest position and directly reporting to the Pharaoh (Genesis 41).

In Genesis 41:45, Joseph married a black Egyptian woman named Asenath — the daughter of the priest Potipherah. They had two sons, Manasseh and Ephraim (Genesis 41:50-52), making their children biracial (half-Israelite and half-Egyptian):

> *"And Pharaoh called Joseph's name Zaphnathpaaneah; and he gave him to wife Asenath the daughter of Potipherah priest of On. And Joseph went out over all the land of Egypt.*
>
> **Genesis 41:45**
>
> *50"And unto Joseph were born two sons before the years of famine came, which Asenath the daughter of Potipherah priest of On bare unto him."*
>
> *51"And Joseph called the name of the firstborn Manasseh: For God, said he, hath made me forget all my toil, and all my father's house.*
>
> *52"And the name of the second called he Ephraim: For*

> *God hath caused me to be fruitful in the land of my affliction."*
>
> **Genesis 41:50-52**

In Genesis chapters 43-45, Joseph finally reconnected with his brothers during a famine period after they traveled from Canaan to Egypt to buy food.

## Joseph Goes Back to Canaan

In Genesis 48, Joseph took his sons, Manasseh and Ephraim, back to Canaan to see their grandfather Jacob (whose name changed to Israel in Genesis 48:2). Jacob was bedridden, nearly blind and nearing his death. Joseph wanted to see his father again and ask for his father's blessings on his own two sons:

> *"And it came to pass after these things, that* one *told Joseph, 'Behold, thy father* is *sick:' and he took with him his two sons, Manasseh and Ephraim.*
>
> *"And* one *told Jacob, and said, 'Behold, thy son Joseph cometh unto thee:' and Israel strengthened himself, and sat upon the bed."*
>
> **Genesis 48: 1-2**

Jacob, now called by the name of Israel, welcomed his biracial grandchildren and blessed them. With this blessing, Manasseh and Ephraim moved into the Hebrew family lineage of their father, Joseph.

> *"And Israel beheld Joseph's sons, and said, 'Who* are *these?'*
>
> *"And Joseph said unto his father, 'They* are *my sons, whom God hath given me in this* place.' *And he said, 'Bring them, I pray thee, unto me, and I will bless them.'"*
>
> **Genesis 48: 8-9**

## Joseph Becomes a Leader in the 12 Tribes of Israel

The twelve sons of Jacob formed the Twelve Tribes of Israel and they appear in several places in the Old Testament. Genesis 29 and

| GENESIS 29-30 | NUMBERS 1 |
| --- | --- |
| Reuben | Reuben |
| Simeon | Simeon |
| Levi | Judah |
| Judah | Dan |
| Dan | Naphtali |
| Naphtali | Gad |
| Gad | Asher |
| Asher | Issachar |
| Issachar | Zebulun |
| Zebulun | Ephraim |
| Joseph | Manasseh |
| Benjamin | Benjamin |

**NOTE:** According to Numbers 1, Levi's name is missing from the Twelve Tribe's listing.

30 contains the 12 sons of Jacob, comprising the original tribes of Israel that included Joseph (see chart).

Later on, Joseph's sons Manasseh and Ephraim received territories and were listed among the 12 leaders (see Numbers 1 listing). As part of the occupation of Israel, each tribe was given a portion of land in their newly acquired homeland.

## Joseph's Sons Emerge As Leaders

Numbers 1:33-34 revealed the emergence of Joseph's sons, Manasseh and Ephraim, as leaders within the 12 Tribes of Israel. Numbers 2:18-20 contains similar information on Joseph's sons listed among the tribe leaders:

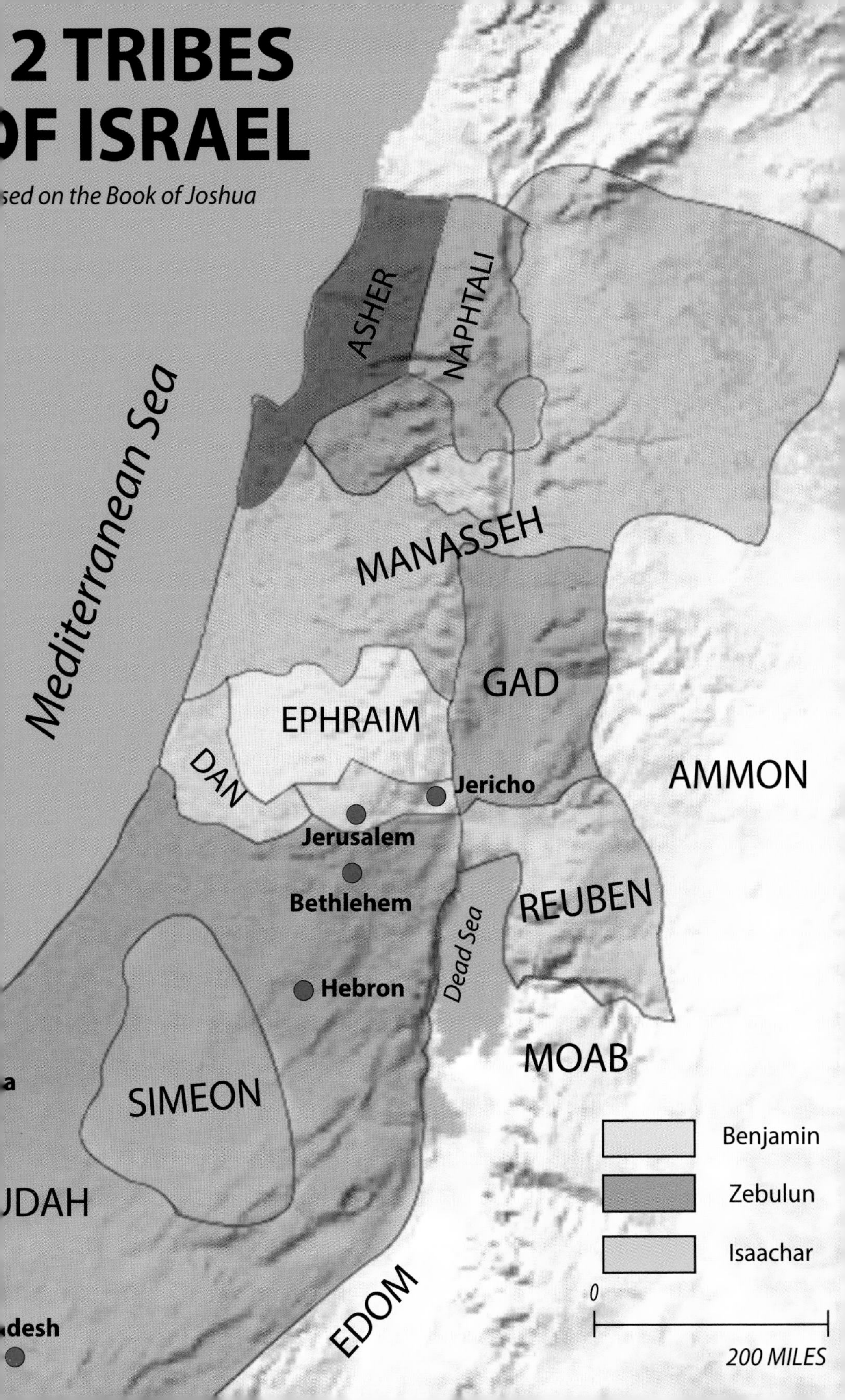
2 TRIBES
F ISRAEL
sed on the Book of Joshua
Mediterranean Sea
ASHER
NAPHTALI
MANASSEH
GAD
EPHRAIM
DAN
Jericho
AMMON
Jerusalem
Bethlehem
Dead Sea
REUBEN
Hebron
MOAB
SIMEON
UDAH
EDOM
adesh
Benjamin
Zebulun
Isaachar
0
200 MILES

*"Those that were numbered of them, even of the tribe of Ephraim, were forty thousand and five hundred.*

*"Of the children of Manasseh, by their generations, after their families, by the house of their fathers, according to the number of the names, from twenty years old and upward, all that were able to go forth to war."*

**Numbers 1:33-34**

Here we have two of the twelve Tribes of Israel led by the biracial sons of Joseph. Manasseh and Ephraim were both half-Egyptian, yet they rose to the ranks of leaders. Their black ancestry carried down through the bloodlines of their Israelite descendants:

*"And Joseph saw Ephraim's children of the third generation: the children also of Machir the son of Manasseh were brought up upon Joseph's knees."*

**Genesis 50:23**

*"And the separate cities for the children of Ephraim were among the inheritance of the children of Manasseh, all the cities with their villages."*

**Joshua 16:9**

**DID YOU KNOW?**

Among the famous descendants of Joseph's son Ephraim was Joshua. Joshua's original name was Oshea, when Moses selected him as one of the 12 spies to travel into Canaan lands initially (Numbers 13:8). Later in Numbers 13:16 and 14:6, Moses called him by the new name Jehoshua (Joshua) and also was the title of the Bible book named in his honor.

## Summary

As one of the most dynamic figures in the Old Testament, Joseph's life intersected with two major Hamite nations, Canaan and Egypt.

From his humble beginnings as a slave, Joseph ascended to one of the highest-ranking leadership roles in Egypt. Moreover, the highlights of Joseph include:

- He lived his early life in Canaan, among black people.
- He later lived in Egypt, a Hamite nation.
- He married a black Egyptian woman.
- His sons were half-Israelite and half-Egyptian, according to their ancestry.

Joseph's sons were the grandchildren of the Israelite patriarch Jacob, who gave them his full blessings. They assimilated fully into the Israelite religion and culture. His sons became leaders within the 12 Tribes of Israel. Their tribes settled in Canaan lands and fought battles against the Canaanite people. Joseph continuously lived his life among black people in black nations.

## Profile of Judah

> *"Judah, thou art he whom thy brethren shall praise: thy hand shall be in the neck of thine enemies; thy father's children shall bow down before thee."*
>
> **Genesis 49:8**

Judah was the fourth of 12 sons of Jacob and his mother was Leah. As the leader of the tribe named after him, Judah was a Semite with the same patriarch lineage as his brother Joseph. Like his brother, Judah's life also intersected regularly with black nations.

Genesis 38:2-5 stated that Judah married a Canaanite woman named Shuah and they had three sons. Judah did not marry a woman from Hebrew-Israelite background as would have been the custom:

> *2"And Judah saw there a daughter of a certain Canaanite, whose name was Shuah; and he took her, and went in*

> *unto her.*
> *3"And she conceived, and bare a son; and he called his name Er.*
>
> *4 "And she conceived again, and bare a son; and she called his name Onan.*
>
> *5 "And she yet again conceived, and bare a son; and called his name Shelah: and he was at Chezib, when she bare him."*
> **Genesis 38:2–5**

Given that Judah was an Israelite and his wife was a Canaanite, their three sons — Er, Onan and Shelah — were biracial (half-Israelite, half-Canaanite). Judah's family were members of Jacob's clan under the Israelite lineage.

**CHALLENGING QUESTION**

Why did Judah marry outside of his nation of Israel, if he was such a prominent member of the 12 Tribes of Israel?

Later in Genesis 38, Judah connected with another Canaanite woman, his daughter-in-law Tamar. She married Judah's oldest son Er, who later died leaving Tamar without any children (Genesis 38:6-7). According to Israelite customs, Judah gave Tamar to his younger son Onan for child-bearing purposes, which Onan refused and he also died.

Later, Tamar hid her true identity and deceived Judah, where he fathered her twin boys, Pharez (Phares in the New Testament) and Zarah (Genesis 38: 11-30). These biracial children were half-Canaanite and half-Israelite and became part of the Israelite nation, based on Judah's designated lineage. Judah's lineage through his son Pharez is noteworthy because it connects to the ancestry of King David, King Solomon and Jesus (see Chapter 11).

In summary, Judah's son from Tamar named Pharez was the father of Esrom and the grandfather of Esrom's son Aram. Pharez, Esrom and Aram, who all had Canaanite ancestry, are part of the genealogy bloodlines for David, Solomon and Jesus. The Canaanites appear in the Davidian line ancestry in at least three generations.

**CHALLENGING QUESTION**

Why is there a pattern of these biracial children becoming part of the nation of Israel, based on their father's heritage?

## Summary

Judah had five sons from two different Canaanite women, Shuah and Tamar. Judah had people with Canaanite ancestry among the members of his tribe, which was one of the 12 Tribes of Israel. Judah is in the genealogy scriptures for the royal family line of David and Jesus. Judah's son Pharez and his descendants are in the ancestral lines of David and Jesus.

## TALKING POINTS

Both Joseph and Judah — leaders in the 12 Tribes of Israel — married Hamite women. Joseph married the Egyptian woman Asenath (Genesis 41:45), the daughter of the priest Potipherah, and had two biracial sons, Manasseh and Ephraim (Genesis 46:20). Judah married the Canaanite woman Shuah (Genesis 38:2) and they had three sons— Er, Onan and Shelah. Judah later had twin sons Pharez and Zarah with his widowed daughter-in-law, the Canaanite Tamar (Genesis 38). Joseph's two biracial sons became leaders of two of the 12 Tribes of Israel.

1.) What do you think about two of the 12 Tribes of Israel being led by the biracial sons of Joseph, Ephraim and Manasseh, who were half-Egyptian and half-Israelite?

2.) What do you think about Judah, one of the leaders in the 12 Tribes of Israel, and all five of his sons were biracial (half Israelite and half-Canaanite)?

# 10

# Moses

*"And the child grew, and she brought him unto Pharaoh's daughter, and he became her son. And she called his name Moses: and she said, 'Because I drew him out of the water.'"*

**Exodus 2:10**

**OBJECTIVE**

This chapter examines the life of the legendary Israelite leader Moses, showing his connection with Hamite people from various backgrounds as he fulfilled his life's mission.

Moses, one of the greatest Israelite leaders of the Old Testament, was a Semite and the great-grandson of Jacob, coming from the Levite tribe of Israel (Shem ->Arphraxad -> Terah -> Abraham -> Isaac -> Jacob -> Levi ->Amran -> Moses). While many movies, paintings and pictures in modern-day culture portray him as a member of the white nations (Japhetites), nothing in the Old Testament supports this belief.

Moreover, some modern historians have referred to Moses as a black man as if he is a Hamite. However, Moses' lineage was not from Ham. Moses, Aaron and their sister Miriam were the children of Amran and Jochebed. Moses' parents' biblical lineage goes back through the Levites and ultimately back to Shem as recorded in the scriptures:

*16 "And these are the names of the sons of Levi according to their generations; Gershon, and Kohath, and Merari: and the years of the life of Levi were an hundred thirty and seven years.*

*17 "The sons of Gershon; Libni, and Shimi, according to their families.*

*18"And the sons of Kohath; Amram, and Izhar, and Hebron, and Uzziel: and the years of the life of Kohath were an hundred thirty and three years.*

*19 "And the sons of Merari; Mahali and Mushi: these are the families of Levi according to their generations.*

*20 "And Amram took him Jochebed his father's sister to wife; and she bare him Aaron and Moses: and the years of the life of Amram were an hundred and thirty and seven years."*

**Exodus 6:16-20**

Moses, his siblings and his parents were all born in Africa. They were part of the generations of Israelites that lived in captivity in Egypt for approximately 400 years. From birth, his childhood and well into his adult life near the age of 40, Moses' only home was on the continent of Africa.

According to Exodus, Pharaoh's daughter found a baby boy floating in the river in a basket. The princess decided to take the baby home and adopt him into her Egyptian family. She gave him the name Moses which meant, "I drew him out of the water (see Exodus 2:10)."

Raised in the home of Pharaoh, Moses did not endure the daily servitude life of the other Israelite people. Moses received training and formal education from the great Egyptian teachers, meaning he was well-equipped to lead the Israelites out of Egypt.

*"And Moses was learned in all the wisdom of the Egyptians, and was mighty in words and in deeds."*

**Acts 7:22**

Egypt led the ancient biblical world in the arts, sciences, religions and medicine. Moses received a superior education usually reserved for the wealthy, affluent and gifted Egyptian people. His training included Egyptian-based instruction on wisdom, knowledge and understanding of the ancient world. Moses was bilingual as he spoke both the Hebrew and Egyptian languages.

Later as an adult, Moses began to move closer to his Hebrew culture and broke away from his Egyptian princely life. He started to join his people, who were enduring a harder life:

> *"By faith Moses, when he was come to years, refused to be called the son of Pharaoh's daughter;*
>
> *"Choosing rather to suffer affliction with the people of God, than to enjoy the pleasures of sin for a season."*
>
> **Hebrews 11:24-25**

**CHALLENGING QUESTION**

Why did Moses move away from the comfort of his Egyptian upbringing and choose to go back to his Israelite heritage?

Later, Moses observed an Egyptian taskmaster beating a Hebrew. Moses was overwhelmed emotionally, killed the Egyptian officer and hid his body:

> *"And it came to pass in those days, when Moses was grown, that he went out unto his brethren, and looked on their burdens: and he spied an Egyptian smiting an Hebrew, one of his brethren.*
>
> *"And he looked this way and that way, and when he saw that there was no man, he slew the Egyptian, and hid him in the sand."*
>
> **Exodus 2:11-12**

When two Hebrew men later confronted Moses about the murder of the Egyptian officer, Moses was afraid for his life and fled Egypt.

> *"And he said, 'Who made thee a prince and a judge over us? intendest thou to kill me, as thou killedst the Egyptian?' And Moses feared, and said, Surely this thing is known.*
>
> *"Now when Pharaoh heard this thing, he sought to slay Moses. But Moses fled from the face of Pharaoh, and dwelt in the land of Midian: and he sat down by a well."*
>
> **Exodus 2:14-15**

Moses fled to Midian, which was located hundreds of miles away in the old Arabian Peninsula (see map). He came upon a group of Midianite girls who were gathering water at a well. While there, he confronted some unruly shepherds and helped the girls collect water for their animals.

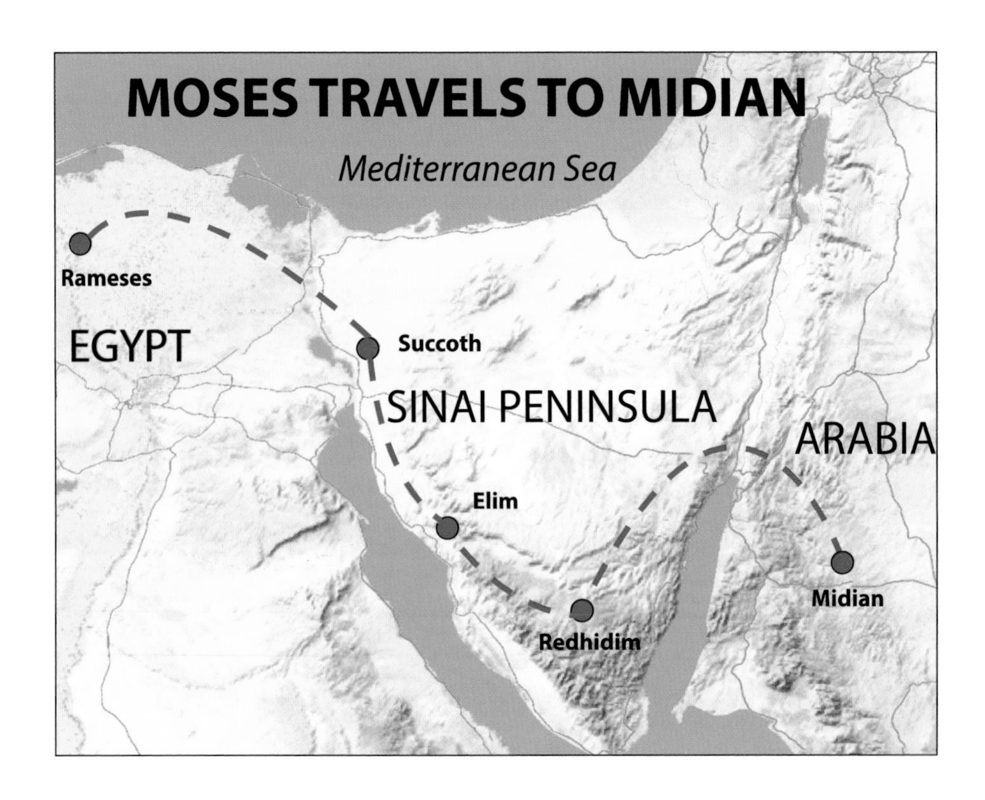

The girls later returned home and gave their father the following report about the stranger who helped them. Their father, Reuel (also called Jethro), served as a priest in Midian.

> *"And when they came to Reuel their father, he said, 'How is it that ye are come so soon today?'*
>
> *"And they said, 'An Egyptian delivered us out of the hand of the shepherds, and also drew water enough for us, and watered the flock.'"*
>
> **Exodus 2:18-19**

The Midianite people were descendants of Shem, the same lineage as Moses. Yet the girls immediately thought Moses was an Egyptian, more specifically a Hamite. The Egyptians during Moses' lifetime were dark-skinned people. According to Genesis 10, they were the descendants of Ham. Moreover, Psalms 78:51, Psalms105:23 and Pslams105:27 referred to Egypt as "the Land of Ham."

## CHALLENGING QUESTION

Why did the Midianite girls think Moses was an Egyptian? Did he speak in an Egyptian dialect? Did he wear the customary Egyptian clothing that the girls observed? Did he possess a dark-skinned complexion like the Egyptians they had seen before?

It's hard to imagine that Moses wore distinctive Egyptian clothing if he had escaped from Egyptian officials. The one characteristic that had to be present would be skin color like the dark-skinned Egyptians. Moses' complexion might have made the girls think he was Egyptian.

While Moses may have had a brown to dark brown complexion (even though he was not a Hamite), his skin tone would support the Midian girls' belief that Moses was an Egyptian.

Moses remained in the land of the Midianites and later married Zipporah, the daughter of Reuel:

> *"And Moses was content to dwell with the man: and he gave Moses Zipporah his daughter."*
>
> **Exodus 2:21**

However, Numbers 12:1 stated that Zipporah was an Ethiopian woman. The Ethiopians are descendants of Ham's son, Cush (see Genesis 10:6):

> *"And Miriam and Aaron spake against Moses because of the Ethiopian woman whom he had married: for he had married an Ethiopian woman."*
>
> **Numbers 12:1**

So why is Zipporah referred to as a Midianite in Exodus 2:21 and an Ethiopian in Numbers 12:1? No one has a complete answer, but in ancient days the designation of "Ethiopian" was often used for many dark-complexioned people who had Hamite ancestry within their bloodlines.

"Ethiopian" became a universal term used for people in the land areas of ancient Africa, parts of Asia and Arabia. The Hamites and Semites mixed continuously, so interracial intermixing was probable involving the Midianites.

For the scope of this book, Numbers 12:1 substantiates Zipporah's ancestral lineage as a Hamite, referring to her as an Ethiopian.

Moses and Zipporah had two sons, Gershom and Eliezer, who were biracial (I Chronicles 23:15). Moses raised Gershom and Eliezer within the Israelite religion and they did not move back into the Ethiopian heritage of their mother.

## Summary

Moses spent his entire life surrounded by black people. The Old Testament shows the connection between the Hamite and Semite nations:

- Moses, his siblings and parents were all born and raised in Egypt, which is in Africa.
- Pharaoh's daughter raised Moses.
- Moses attended excellent schools in Egypt and had access to Egypt's superior knowledge and resources.
- Moses lived the first 40 years of his life among black people.
- Moses married a black Ethiopian woman and fathered biracial sons.

## TALKING POINTS

Moses' life was interwoven around black people. This iconic Israelite leader also married the Ethiopian woman Zipporah (Numbers 12:1). Moses and Zipporah had two biracial children, Gershom and Eliezer (I Chronicles 23:15). Moreover, Moses' life further builds the case of the ongoing prominence and influence of black nations among the Israelites in the Old Testament. The story of Moses would seem incomplete without his constant interaction with the Hamite black nations.

1.) Why are Hollywood movies, Eurocentric books, paintings and pictures obsessed with making Moses (who was Asiatic/Semite) a member of the white nations of people?

2.) Why did this iconic Israelite leader marry Zipporah, who was outside of the Hebrew faith?

# 11

# Solomon

*"Then sat Solomon upon the throne of David, his father; and his kingdom was established greatly."*

**1 Kings 2:12**

**OBJECTIVE**

Solomon's high level of wisdom allowed him to build strong relationships with foreign Hamite countries. He used these alliances for personal, political and business reasons. This chapter examines his continuous connections to Hamite nations and their people.

Solomon, the son of the legendary King David and Bathsheba, is considered one of the greatest kings of Israel in the Old Testament. Solomon ruled a unified Israel that included both northern and southern regions from approximately 970 to 931 B.C. Known for his exceptional wisdom and strong government administration abilities, Solomon also was known for his romantic adventures with numerous women, especially those from foreign countries.

This chapter will review Solomon's life through historical lenses with 1 Kings and 1 and 2 Samuel as the source material. Subsections will include a discussion of Solomon's paternal and maternal lineage, a review of Solomon's life and an overview of building the Great Temple.

## King David

The stories of Solomon's father King David are told in 1 Samuel, 2 Samuel and 1 Kings. Starting with his famous battle with Goliath as a boy, David's bravery in countless battles led to his rise as king of Israel. During his estimated 40-year reign (1010 B.C. to 970 B.C.), David's leadership skills helped shape the Israelite nation.

In his youth, David was a shepherd and the youngest son of Jesse. 1 Samuel 16:12-13 talked about God's anointment of David as the future king of Israel. 1 Samuel 16:12 referred to the young lad's physical appearance when he met the prophet, Samuel. This verse made specific mention of David's complexion as "ruddy," which means "red" or "reddish:"

> *"And he sent and brought him in. Now he was ruddy, and withal of a beautiful countenance and goodly to look to. And the Lord said, 'Arise, anoint him, for this is he.'"*
>
> *"Then Samuel took the horn of oil, and anointed him in the midst of his brethren: and the Spirit of the LORD came upon David from that day forward. So Samuel rose up, and went to Ramah."*
>
> **1 Samuel 16:12-13**

Modern biblical scholars occasionally dismiss the Bible's direct reference to David's skin complexion. However, this was one of the few Old Testament specific references to a person's skin color.

Another different, yet noteworthy topic, involves David's genealogy known as the Davidic Line or the House of David. David was a Semite, meaning his lineage traced back through Abraham and ultimately to Noah's son Shem, father of the Asiatic nations, as chronicled in Matthew 1:

> *2"Abraham begat Isaac; and Isaac begat Jacob; and Jacob begat Judah and his brethren;*
>
> *3"And Judah begat Phares and Zara of Thamar; and Phares begat Esrom; and Esrom begat Aram;*

*4 "And Aram begat Aminadab; and Aminadab begat Naasson; and Naasson begat Salmon;*

*5 "And Salmon begat Booz of Rachab; and Booz begat Obed of Ruth; and Obed begat Jesse;*

*6 "And Jesse begat David the king; and David the king begat Solomon of (Bathsheba) that had been the wife of Urias."*

**Matthew 1: 2-6**

David's genealogy in Matthew 1 also included the recorded genealogy lines for Jesus Christ, who came through the same recorded bloodlines as David:

*"The book of the generation of Jesus Christ, the son of David, the son of Abraham."*

**Matthew 1:1**

*"And Eliud begat Eleazar; and Eleazar begat Matthan; and Matthan begat Jacob;"*

*"And Jacob begat Joseph the husband of Mary, of whom was born Jesus, who is called Christ."*

**Matthew 1:15-16**

What is noteworthy is that David and Jesus' genealogy also included several people of Canaanite ancestry and at least one person of Moabite ancestry:

- Phares, the son of Judah, and the Canaanite Thamar, making Phares biracial (Matthew 1:2).
- Esrom, the son of Phares, had Canaanite ancestry (Matthew 1:2).
- Rachab or Rahab, a Canaanite woman who was the mother of Booz (Matthew 1:5).
- Ruth, a Moabite who was the mother of Obed (Matthew 1:5).

## Bathsheba

Solomon's mother, Bathsheba, was introduced into the Bible as a married woman upon whom David gazed while she was bathing:

> *"And it came to pass in an evening tide, that David arose from off his bed, and walked upon the roof of the king's house: and from the roof he saw a woman washing herself; and the woman was very beautiful to look upon.*
>
> *"And David sent and inquired after the woman. And one said, 'Is not this Bathsheba, the daughter of Eliam, the wife of Uriah the Hittite?'"*
>
> **2 Samuel 11:2-3**

In these verses, the Bible revealed background information on Bathsheba on two important historical points: she was the wife of Uriah the Hittite and the daughter of Eliam.

The ancient Hittites were members of Ham's family genealogy tree. Ham's son Canaan was the father of Heth, who was listed as the ancestor of the Hittites (Noah -> Ham -> Canaan ->Heth -> Hittites). The Hittites were also members of the more massive Canaanite nation since Heth's father was Canaan.

It is possible that if Bathsheba's husband was a Hittite, she also might have been a Hittite. While her ethnic background is not clear, there are general thoughts that Bathsheba was a Hittite or possessed Canaanite ancestry, meaning she belonged to the family tree of Ham. Modern history tries to move her away from Hamite genealogy, but the biblical records don't support this theory.

Moreover, why was a Hittite (Uriah) listed as a prominent member in King David's army? The Hittites were part of the larger Canaanite nation. Biblical stories indicate the Israelites despised the Canaanites and were instructed by God to kill them all (Deuteronomy 20:16-17, Joshua 3:10). Yet centuries later, here was a Hittite (Canaanite) enlisted prominently in the Israelite army and fighting alongside Israelite soldiers.

**CHALLENGING QUESTION**

For David to know Uriah's identity, it would imply Uriah had a certain rank in David's army. How did a Hittite rise to such prominence in the Israelite army?

Second Samuel 11-12 tells that Bathsheba had a romantic relationship with David and became pregnant. Later, David had her husband sent to the front battle lines where Uriah died in military action. David married Bathsheba and they had two sons— one who died as an infant and Solomon.

The second historical point involves Bathsheba's father, Eliam, whose ancestry is listed in 2 Samuel 11:3 and 2 Samuel 23:34:

> *"Eliphelet the son of Ahasbai, the son of the Maachathite, Eliam the son of Ahithophel the Gilonite."*
>
> **2 Samuel 23:34**

Bathsheba's grandfather Ahithophel was from the town of Giloh, located in Canaan lands. The original Canaanites were not expelled from this city once the Israelites took control of the region (Joshua 15:51). There is debate as to whether Eliam and Ahithophel were possibly Israelites with Canaanite ancestry. This question arises because of the constant interracial mixing and marriages between early Israelites and Canaanites.

As noted throughout this book, Hamites and Semites always mixed and married each other throughout the Old Testament era. Moreover, Bathsheba's father and grandfather's backgrounds and her marriage to Uriah go back to a connection with Canaanite people.

**CHALLENGING QUESTION**

David and Solomon's ancestries most likely contained Hamite bloodlines. Why is this information not openly discussed in today's world?

## Solomon's Life

After David's death, Solomon became king of Israel. Scholars believe that he reigned approximately 970 to 931 B.C., hundreds of years before the emergence of Greece and Rome.

First Kings 11:1-3 cited the multitude of wives and women in Solomon's life, including women from foreign lands. The scriptures also mentioned God's warning for Solomon not to marry women from foreign nations:

> *1 "But King Solomon loved many strange women, together with the daughter of Pharaoh, women of the Moabites, Ammonites, Edomites, Zidonians, and Hittites;*
>
> *2 "Of the nations concerning which the LORD said unto the children of Israel, Ye shall not go in to them, neither shall they come in unto you: for surely they will turn away your heart after their gods: Solomon clave unto these in love."*
>
> *3 "And he had seven hundred wives, princesses, and three hundred concubines: and his wives turned away his heart."*
>
> **1 Kings 11:1-3**

The following chart traces the ancestral nations for the women cited in 1 Kings 11:1 (left and center columns). The right column traces the women's ancestral nations from Noah's sons, as detailed in Genesis 10. Scholars determined Solomon's marriage practices were politically motivated to build allies with neighboring countries for

| NAME | BIBLICAL NATION | ANCESTRY FROM NOAH'S SONS |
|---|---|---|
| Pharaoh's daughter | Egypt | Ham |
| Moabites | Moab | Shem |
| Ammonites | Ammon | Shem |
| Edomites | Edom | Shem |
| Zidonians | Zidon (Sidon) | Ham |
| Hittites | Canaan | Ham |

the advancement of Israel. While that may be a sound assumption, it is noticeable that half of the women listed in 1 Kings 11 were from Hamite nations. This citing reinforces how visible and prominent black nations were during Solomon's reign if the political motivation theory is correct.

Moreover, there was also a noticeable pattern of Solomon choosing women from both Hamite and Semite nations. None of these scriptures regarding Solomon's many women mentioned any women from biblical white nations (Japhetites). Solomon's story — like many Old Testament leaders — dealt with an Israelite leader that had continuous interactions with the Hamite- black nations.

These interactions included political alignments, economic commerce, military encounters and intermarrying. What also is noticeable is there is little to no recorded interaction with the Japhetites.

One of Solomon's most famous connections with a Hamite nation and its female ruler was with the Ethiopian queen Makeda, as recorded in 1 Kings 10:1-13 and 2 Chronicles 9:1-12. They had a son named Menelik, who later became an outstanding ruler of the Ethiopian Empire and continued the royal bloodlines, which ruled Ethiopia until the late 20th century A.D.

**CHALLENGING QUESTION**

Why did Solomon choose to marry women from foreign lands, with an emphasis on Hamite (black) women?

**CHALLENGING QUESTION**

Why aren't Japhetite (white) women listed among Solomon's wives and mistresses?

## Solomon Builds the Great Temple

The Bible talked of David's desire to build a magnificent temple in Jerusalem (see 1 Kings 8:17 and 1 Chronicles 22:7). David did not fulfill this goal in his lifetime and the task passed down to his son Solomon.

Facing this daunting assignment, Solomon went to the Sidonians — the descendants of Canaan's son, Sidon (also spelled as Zidon) — to help him build it. As told in 1 Chronicles 22, Solomon demonstrated a unique strategy by reaching out to King Hiram for assistance. The Sidonians were part of the overall Canaanite nation, thus making them part of Ham's family tree (Noah -> Ham -> Canaan ->Sidon -> Sidonians/ Zidonians). The book of Joshua referred to Zidon (Sidon) with reverence:

> *"And Hebron, and Rehob, and Hammon, and Kanah, even unto great Zidon."*
>
> **Joshua 19:28**

**CHALLENGING QUESTION**

Why would King Solomon, ruler of Israel, reach out to a Canaanite king for assistance with building God's temple?

**CHALLENGING QUESTION**

Didn't the Israelites consider the Canaanites pagans, idol worshippers and unclean living people, as cited in Deuteronomy 20:16-17 and Joshua 3:10?

## The Phoenicians

While the Bible referred to Hiram and the Sidonians, the people living in the cities of Sidon and Tyre took on a new regional name — the Phoenicians. During the reigns of David and Solomon, the

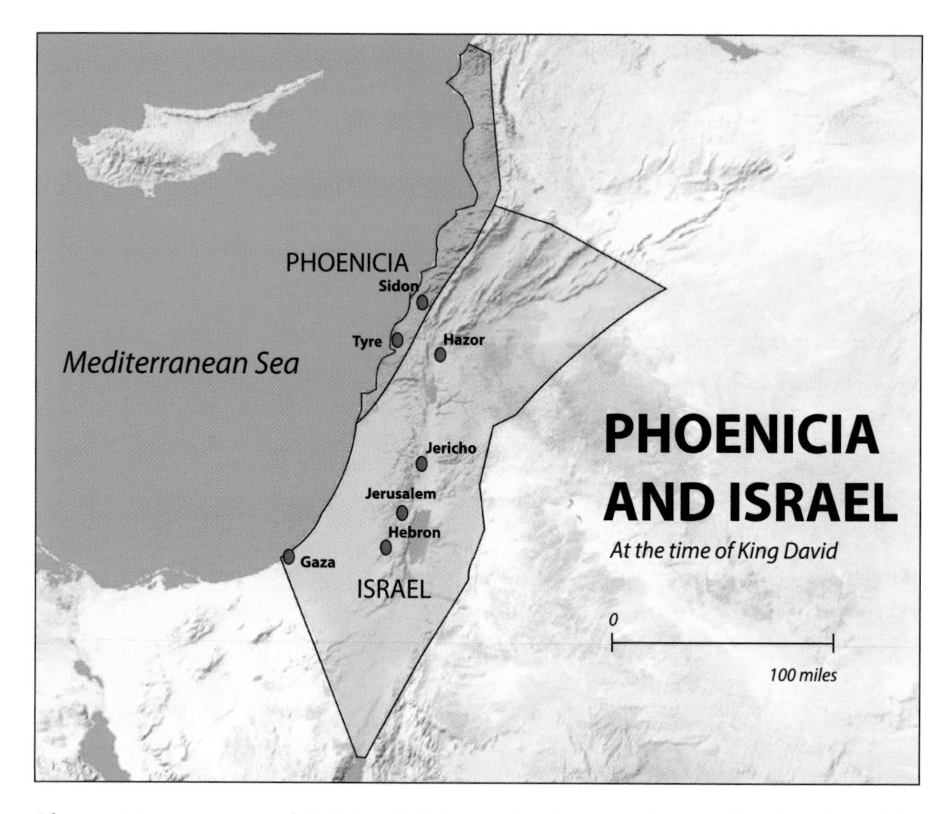


Phoenicians were a highly visible and advanced people that lived in the northern regions of the old Canaan lands called Phoenicia, known as present-day Lebanon (see map). For the context of this chapter, the words "Sidon," "Zidon" and "Phoenicia" are synonymous.

Hiram ruled over Tyre and was influential over Sidon. Both ancient Canaanite cities were situated near the mountain regions near the Mediterranean Sea. During the Old Testament era, Tyre and Sidon were leading cities for commercial trading with neighboring countries, including Israel.

The Phoenicians were skilled seamen and navigated the entire Mediterranean Sea in their highly crafted boats, setting up regional business zones and trading posts. They were very engaged in commercial trade and sold their goods throughout the region, especially their renowned purple cloths. The Phoenicians were highly skilled builders of magnificent statues, monuments and large buildings.

The Phoenicians were the descendants of the ancient Canaanite nation, which was the source of their knowledge in commercial trade and building. Additionally, the Phoenicians were part of the Hamite family, which included the Ethiopians and Egyptians, as cited in Genesis 10.

## Solomon and Hiram Negotiate

Hiram had business relationships with David that continued during the reign of Solomon. 1 Kings 5:1-12 provides background information for this story.

The first five verses review Hiram and Solomon's meeting as Solomon unveiled his vision to build the temple. The passages show Hiram's respect for Solomon's father, David, and confirm Hiram and David's previous diplomatic interactions.

> *1 "And Hiram king of Tyre sent his servants unto Solomon; for he had heard that they had anointed him king in the room of his father: for Hiram was ever a lover of David.*
>
> *2 "And Solomon sent to Hiram, saying,*
>
> *3 'Thou knowest how that David my father could not build an house unto the name of the LORD his God for the wars which were about him on every side, until the LORD put them under the soles of his feet.*
>
> *4 'But now the LORD my God hath given me rest on every side, so that there is neither adversary nor evil occurrent.*
>
> *5 'And, behold, I purpose to build an house unto the name of the LORD my God,' as the LORD spake unto David my father, saying, 'Thy son, whom I will set upon thy throne in thy room, he shall build an house unto my name.'"*
>
> **1 Kings 5:1-5**

Moreover, the verses tell of Solomon's request to Hiram for assistance in building the Great Temple in Jerusalem. It was interesting that Solomon would go outside of the Israelite nation for essential help with the temple.

## Building the Great Temple

Continuing in 1 Kings 5: 6-10, Hiram and Solomon defined the temple's need for distinctive cedar tree timber from the Sidonians. They also agreed that skilled Sidonian workers would cut and transport the wood to Jerusalem. The Sidonians had engineering techniques for floating large timbers through the rivers and seas for their final destination to awaiting customers such as Israel. The Sidonians were highly skilled builders and workers who had a known reputation throughout the region.

In exchange for the Sidonians' timber and labor, Hiram negotiated with Solomon to supply his nation with grain and food supplies. The trade agreement demonstrated the Sidonians' skills in economic commerce and negotiations, construction, engineering and logistics:

> *6 "'Now therefore command thou that they hew me cedar trees out of Lebanon; and my servants shall be with thy servants: and unto thee will I give hire for thy servants according to all that thou shalt appoint: for thou knowest that there is not among us any that can skill to hew timber like unto the Zidonians.'"*
>
> *7 "And it came to pass, when Hiram heard the words of Solomon, that he rejoiced greatly, and said, 'Blessed be the LORD this day, which hath given unto David a wise son over this great people.'"*
>
> *8 "And Hiram sent to Solomon, saying, 'I have considered the things which thou sentest to me for: and I will do all thy desire concerning timber of cedar, and concerning timber of fir.*
>
> *9 "'My servants shall bring them down from Lebanon unto the sea: and I will convey them by sea in floats unto the place that thou shalt appoint me, and will cause them to be discharged there, and thou shalt receive them: and thou shalt accomplish my desire, in giving food for my household.'"*

> *10 "So Hiram gave Solomon cedar trees and fir trees according to all his desire."*
>
> **1 Kings 5:6-10**

## CHALLENGING QUESTION

Why did Solomon go to King Hiram to import skilled workers to build the temple in Jerusalem?

Hiram and Solomon consummated the business and financial portions of their trade agreement in 1 Kings 5:11-12. Additionally, the kings developed a peace treaty between their nations.

> *"And Solomon gave Hiram twenty thousand measures of wheat for food to his household, and twenty measures of pure oil: thus gave Solomon to Hiram year by year. "And the LORD gave Solomon wisdom, as he promised him: and there was peace between Hiram and Solomon; and they two made a league together."*
>
> **1 Kings 5:11-12**

The Sidonian workers traveled to Jerusalem on work assignments that were recorded in the Bible. They led the highly skilled tasks needed to build the Great Temple, as listed in 1 Kings: 5-6. They led the work efforts along with the Israelites to measure, cut, extract and transport the necessary stones from rock quarries to the temples' location.

> *"And the king commanded, and they brought great stones, costly stones, and hewed stones, to lay the foundation of the house."*
>
> *"And Solomon's builders and Hiram's builders did hew them, and the stonesquarers: so they prepared timber and stones to build the house."*
>
> **1 Kings 5:17-18**

The Sidonian workers led the effort to carve intricate designs on temple panels, doors and walls, with Solomon serving as project manager:

> *27"And he set the cherubims within the inner house: and they stretched forth the wings of the cherubims, so that the wing of the one touched the* one *wall, and the wing of the other cherub touched the other wall; and their wings touched one another in the midst of the house."*
>
> *28"And he overlaid the cherubims with gold."*
>
> *29"And he carved all the walls of the house round about with carved figures of cherubims and palm trees and open flowers, within and without."*
>
> *32"The two doors also were of olive tree; and he carved upon them carvings of cherubims and palm trees and open flowers, and overlaid them with gold, and spread gold upon the cherubims, and upon the palm trees."*
>
> **1 Kings 6: 27-29, 32**

In 2 Chronicles, Solomon asked Hiram to send a top-rated Phoenician artisan for the particular design work needed for the temple:

> *"Send me now therefore a man cunning to work in gold, and in silver, and in brass, and in iron, and in purple, and crimson, and blue, and that can skill to grave with the cunning men that* are *with me in Judah and in Jerusalem, whom David my father did provide."*
>
> **2 Chronicles 2:7**

Hiram fulfilled Solomon's request with a highly skilled Phoenician artisan to perform the intricate carvings, metal workings and interior design.

**NOTE:** King Hiram's name is spelled "Huram" in 2 Chronicles; the artisan listed in 2 Chronicles was also named "Huram."

> *11"Then Huram the king of Tyre answered in writing, which he sent to Solomon, Because the LORD hath loved his people, he hath made thee king over them."*

*13"And now I have sent a cunning man, endued with understanding, of Huram my father's,"*

*14"The son of a woman of the daughters of Dan, and his father* was *a man of Tyre, skillful to work in gold, and in silver, in brass, in iron, in stone, and in timber, in purple, in blue, and in fine linen, and in crimson; also to grave any manner of graving, and to find out every device which shall be put to him, with thy cunning men, and with the cunning men of my lord David, thy father."*

**2 Chronicles 2:11, 13-14**

*11"And Huram made the pots, and the shovels, and the basons. And Huram finished the work that he was to make for king Solomon for the house of God;"*

*22"And the snuffers, and the basons, and the spoons, and the censers,* of *pure gold: and the entry of the house, the inner doors thereof for the most holy* place, *and the doors of the house of the temple,* were of *gold."*

**2 Chronicles 4:11, 22**

According to 1 Kings 6:2-3, the Great Temple was 60 cubits long, 20 cubits wide and 30 cubits high; the porch (the lobby area entering the temple) was 20 cubits long, 20 cubits wide and 10 cubits high. Historians estimate a cubit to be roughly 18 inches in length.

According to 1 Kings 9, it took 20 years to build the temple and the royal palace that the Israelite and Phoenician men worked on together. The following verses detailed the continued commerce and trade between the Israelites and the Phoenicians:

*"And it came to pass at the end of twenty years, when Solomon had built the two houses, the house of the LORD, and the king's house,"*

"Now *Hiram the king of Tyre had furnished Solomon with cedar trees and fir trees, and with gold, according to all his desire, that then king Solomon gave Hiram twenty cities in the land of Galilee."*

**1 Kings 9:10-11**

The Bible also recorded information on the strong fleet of ships that Hiram and the Phoenicians maintained. These citations further document the power, prestige and wealth of biblical-era black nations.

> *"And Hiram sent in the navy his servants, shipmen that had knowledge of the sea, with the servants of Solomon."*
>
> **1 Kings 9:27**

> *"And the navy also of Hiram, that brought gold from Ophir, brought in from Ophir great plenty of almug trees, and precious stones."*
>
> **1 Kings 10:11**

Solomon exhibited extraordinary vision, planning and administrative duties in building the Great Temple. For approximately 20 years, he oversaw a multitude of Israelite and foreign workers in the areas of architecture, engineering and interior design. Solomon's long-term strategic planning skills allowed the project to continue while he also ran Israel's daily business and governmental affairs of the country. Ultimately, Solomon's negotiations with Hiram proved highly beneficial to the completion of this magnificent temple.

## Summary

Matthew 1 supports that Solomon was a man of mixed ancestral bloodlines due to his Canaanite and Moabite ancestors. Solomon embraced both his Semite and Hamite heritage, as evidenced through his marriages, personal relationships with Hamite women and his alliances with black nations for ongoing commerce and trade. Regional countries such as Egypt, Ethiopia and Phoenicia acknowledged Solomon's wisdom and diplomatic skills.

Additionally, Solomon maintained a peaceful existence with his neighboring countries while promoting and sustaining Israel to a higher quality of prominence and economic livelihood. Ultimately, Solomon's extraordinary wisdom allowed him to recruit Phoenician engineers and artisans to build the Great Temple of Jerusalem.

While history chronicles Solomon's leadership and wisdom, this chapter also shows how the black presence was evident. Throughout the chapters, the Hamite people-black nations continued to march across the biblical pages and participate in the important stories and events. The black nations were too developed and advanced for the Israelites to ignore their presence.

The Israelites regularly interacted with the Hamites and often were dependent on the black nations to help them in their overall advancement. The story of Solomon followed this pattern as he sought interaction, alliance and support from various black nations as he developed Israel.

## TALKING POINTS

There is a strong belief that King Solomon's mother, Bathsheba, was a Canaanite — leading to the possibility that Solomon was biracial. Additionally, the genealogy for David and Solomon in Matthew 1 contains Canaanite and Moabite lineage in their ancestry. Solomon's decision to use Phoenicians (Canaanites) as engineers, architects and craftsmen to build the Great Temple in Jerusalem contradicts the misconception that the Canaanites were not considered significant contributors in the Old Testament.

1.) How do you feel about the possibility that King Solomon might have been bi-racial (part-Israelite, part-Canaanite)?

2.) Why do you think there is a mixture of ethnic nations (Hebrew/Israelite, Canaanite and Moabite) contained in the Matthew1 genealogy for David and Solomon?

3.) Why do you think King Solomon chose foreign -pagan worshipping workers (engineers, architects and craftsman) to build The Great Temple in Jerusalem?

4.) What would cause high-profile Old Testament Hebrew leaders such as King Solomon to marry Hamite women?

# A Message to the Descendants of Ham

Our ancient ancestors left us cultural roadmaps and historical blueprints of the success that occurred when black nations operated with dynamic vision, unity, creativity and excellence. The Old Testament writers acknowledged the existence and prominence of these black nations.

For example, the fundamentals of writing came from the ancient Sumerians of Mesopotamia, Egyptians and the Ethiopians. The development of writing was but one of many significant contributions made by these ancient nations. As mentioned, black nations were leaders in the arts, sciences, commerce, and engineering long before the emergence of the Greeks and Romans.

These nations left a historical foundation and platform that we can stand on with pride, lean on during difficult times and plant our visionary seeds for the future. The participation of black nations in the development of ancient civilization should be studied to understand the times when they stood on top of the world and led the way for other nations.

During recent centuries, descendants of Ham have borrowed from other cultural models — most notably European models – as the basis of history, politics, religion, business and other socioeconomic models not necessarily created for our benefit. Without using our historical platform, we have to borrow from and imitate other groups' platforms. Imitating other groups' history and culture is not a solid long-term strategy for any race of people.

The study of ancient times will help us to acquire the needed fundamentals of our history. We should study our history from various periods and the collection of people involved during those time frames. However, we can't dwell just on the A.D. period for our history discussions, because there are more than 6,000 years of our rich history in the B.C. period where black nations dominated.

The timeline of these ancient black nations was so long ago that the modern world often doesn't see it as relevant. Well, we MUST make it relevant because it is our history and our people. Here are the benefits of studying ancient black civilizations:

- You grow your history.
- You develop your culture.
- You strengthen your people.
- You add humanitarian value.
- You move from unaware to awareness.
- You enhance your cultural vision and unity expands.
- You become less culturally dependent on other groups.

We no longer can allow other groups to take our history, translate it with different characters and events, then claim it as their own while feeding us toxic stories of a non-achieving black race. Global survival requires us to move forward together with minimal jealousy while using the self principles to achieve our renewed greatness. These self principles include the cultural disciplines of self-destiny, self-sustaining, self-control, self-preservation and self-direction.

We must interconnect nationally and internationally and have a deeper appreciation for Africa. As long as we remain culturally devoid and are not aware of our history, we will continue to be victims of mental oppression. The physical chains may not be there, but remnants of the mental bondage remain.

Together, let's stand responsibly and productively on the brilliant legacy of our ancestors. Let's hold our heads high and carry radiant smiles of greatness. Historical knowledge also promotes healthy cultural esteem because these two components work well together.

Peace be unto everyone!

**Ronald Harrill**

# BIBLIOGRAPHY

The Holy Bible, King James Version. Cambridge Edition: 1769; King James Bible Online, 2020. www.kingjamesbibleonline.org.

Brand, Chad; Draper, Charles; England, Archie (2003). Holman Illustrated Bible Dictionary. Nashville, TN: Holman Bible Publishers.

Green, Richard L. (1988). A Salute to Historic African Kings and Queens. Chicago, IL: Empak Enterprises, Inc.

Hansberry, William Leo (1981). Africa and Africans as Seen by Classical Writers. Vol. 2. Washington, D.C.: Howard University Press.

Houston, Drusilla Dunjee (1985). Wonderful Ethiopians of the Ancient Cushite Empire. Baltimore, MD: Black Classics Press. Original work published in 1926 (Oklahoma City, OK: The Universal Publishing Co.).

Jackson, John G. (1939). Ethiopia and the Origin of Civilization. Baltimore, MD: Black Classic Press.

Josephus, Flavius; Whiston, William (translator); Boer, Paul A. (editor) (2014). The Antiquities of the Jews: Vol. I (Books I - X). Scotts Valley, CA: CreateSpace Independent Publishing Platform.

Rogers, J.A. World's Great Men of Color. Vol. 1 (1972). New York, NY: McMillan Publishing.

The Holy Bible, Black Heritage Edition: King James Version (1976). Nashville, TN: Today, Inc.

Supreme Understanding (2013). When the World Was Black – The Untold History of the World's First Civilizations. Atlanta, GA: Supreme Design Publishing.

Williams, Chancellor (1976). The Destruction of Black Civilization: Great Issues of a Race from 4500 B.C. to 2000 A.D. 13th ed. Chicago, IL: Third World Press.